PRAISE FOR *BEING*

"Because this book is a tapestry of beautiful and authentic self-story-telling, the reader is invited to safely journey inside their own inner terrain. Tremendously helpful!"

PAUL YOUNG, AUTHOR OF *THE SHACK*

"As Karl's story confirms, finding our worth, value and security in the Love that calls us into 'being' actually frees and opens the adventure of 'becoming.'"

PAUL D. FITZGERALD, D.MIN., HEARTCONNEXION SEMINARS

"In a sea of toxic masculinity, *Being* offers another way to engage the spiritual life for men and others. Karl's demonstration of honest vulnerability and change will live deep in your heart as you begin your own journey."

REV. DR. KATY E. VALENTINE, AUTHOR AND PODCASTER

"In telling his sacred story of family dysfunction, personal rejection, fear and anger, and slow progressive healing, Karl Forehand forces us to look within and find our own shadow. And in the process, he reminds us of who we really are in relation to our Source."

REV. DR. MICHAEL J. CHRISTENSEN, PH.D., ACADEMIC DEAN AND PROFESSOR OF THEOLOGY, NORTHWIND INSTITUTE | SEMINARY

"*Being* is not just a book you read, *Being* is a book that reads you."

NORA SOPHIA

"Karl Forehand is offering a vulnerable window into the journey many church people are finding themselves on, after years of being chained to certainty."

ALANA LEVANDOSKI, SONGWRITER, RECORDING ARTIST, PRODUCER, OF POINT VIERGE: THOMAS MERTON'S JOURNEY IN SONG

"*Being* encourages us to look within. A balm for the harried soul, I recommend this book to anyone craving peace but unsure of where to find it."

CHRISTOPHER EAKER, SPIRITUAL DETECTOR, STEPPING STONES LIFE

"There is no way to not hear God in the voice of an authentic word and Karl's here is just that—authentic."

SETH PRICE, HOST OF THE "CAN I SAY THIS AT CHURCH?" PODCAST

"Karl Forehand helps the reader discover our true, eternal being-nature vs. doing-nature, which diminish its unhealthy power over our minds."

ANITA GRACE BROWN, AUTHOR OF *KAMAKAZI YOGI*

"For those like me who have bottomed out on distraction and are ready to go deeper, Karl's journey is a beautiful path into authenticity and wholeness. He's a kind and seasoned guide!"

BRAD JERSAK, AUTHOR OF *A MORE CHRISTLIKE WAY*

"Karl Forehand invites us to journey with him and gives us a bird's eye view of a journey toward wholehearted living and an invitation for the reader to embark on their own path toward self-discovery and wholeness."

MARY JEPPSEN, PH.D.

BEING

A Journey Toward Presence and Authenticity

Karl Forehand

All rights reserved. No part of this book may be used or reproduced, stored in a retrieval system, or transmitted in any form or by any means, electronic, mechanical, photocopying, recording, scanning, or otherwise, without written permission from the publisher except in the case of brief quotations embodied in critical articles and reviews. Permission for wider usage of this material can be obtained through Shaia-Sophia House by emailing permission@shaiasophiahouse.com.

Copyright © 2021 by Karl J. Forehand.

First Edition

Cover design and layout by Rafael Polendo (polendo.net)
Cover image courtesy of GraphicStock.com

ISBN 978-1-7348234-6-2

This volume is printed on acid free paper and meets ANSI Z39.48 standards.

Printed in the United States of America

Published by Shaia-Sophia House
An imprint of Quoir
San Antonio, Texas, USA

www.ShaiaSophiaHouse.com

To my companion on the Being Journey,
Laura Forehand.

TABLE OF CONTENTS

Foreword 8
Introduction. 11

Part I—Don't Waste a Good Crisis. 15
   What is Happening? 16
   The Weekend 19
   My History with Rejection 24
   Going Back to Work 31
   Leaving Home. 34
   It All Happened in a Recliner 37
   Telling My Story 44

Part II—Going Deeper. 49
   Going Deeper with My Fear 50
   Going Deeper with My Anger. 56
   Going Deeper with My Bypassing. 62
   Going Deeper with my Voice 67

    Going Deeper with my Critic 75
    Going Deeper with my Pain 83

Part III—Learning to Be 87
    Being with Crisis. 88
    Being with Prophets and Poets 96
    Being with Community. 101
    Being with Nature. 110
    Being with Pain. 116
    Being with Solitude. 123
    Being with Uncertainty 129
    Being with the Divine 135
    Being with the Ignorant 142
    Being with My Dog. 149
    Being with My Body 154

Epilogue—Bravery and Vulnerability 158

FOREWORD

We are human beings, who have become excellent human doers, caught in the maze of perpetual distractions. The constant busyness, diversions, entertainment, societal fires constantly needing to be put out, relationship problems, work issues, emails, politics, perpetually theologizing, and obsessive scrolling and posting on social media is dizzying and disorienting. How can we not abnormally acquire ADHD living in our hustle-and-bustle culture? We are simply not designed for the fast, frenetic, and chaotic pace at which we are moving, and it is taking a toll on us. Not only is there an epidemic of insomnia, ulcers, spiritual numbness, and anxiety disorders but busyness is also affecting our core relationships. When afflicted with hurry sickness and lured by every sweet siren of excessive stimuli, giving people, God, and even ourselves undivided attention and presence is next to impossible.

We are also hooked on our gadgets. We have become so addicted to technology that we have developed a phenomenon called phantom vibration syndrome (PVS). PVS occurs when we are so hypervigilant that we hurriedly check our cell phones because we felt the phone vibrate or thought we heard it ring, but, in reality, nobody texted, sent a Facebook message, or called us. It was all in our anxious imagination. PVS is not the only cost to us for being saturated in technology and social media.

Although Facebook, Twitter, Instagram, Pinterest, Google+, and the like can be great ways to connect with others, they cannot adequately provide the type of intimacy and face-to-face presence that people crave. Social networking, and technology in general, does provide some benefits, though. It can be a blessing when you are having a difficult night and need an encouraging word. But as great as such an experience is, it is not enough. Our addiction to technology is robbing us from learning how to *be* with God, ourselves, and our neighbors.

Many of us are also plagued with perfectionism. Our culture elevates strong, sexy, vibrant, rich, and plastic over weak, average, weary, poor, and wrinkled. We are trying to reach some perfect and successful destination, but it is always illusory. We feel that if we can just attain the holy grail of success, our lives would be perfect. Unfortunately, there is a cost to spinning out of control on that hamster wheel to nowhere. Depression, addictions, eating disorders, workaholism, and an aversion to natural human emotions, such as sadness, shame, and fear, are some of the many consequences that have their roots in a perfectionistic culture.

Hidden within the word *perfectionism*, at least phonetically, is the word *shun*, which is a constant reminder of the unfortunate consequence of trying to be perfect. I like to think of *perfectionism* as *perfect*-shun-*ism*.

When we shun somebody, we keep away from, hide from, or avoid that person. We, who are affected by perfect*shun*ism tend to avoid or shun anything that appears to be broken, incomplete, raw, and imperfect. Perfect*shun*ism invariably keeps us from listening to the brokenness within ourselves and others, and it keeps others from engaging with and listening to us. It stops us from knowing each other and ourselves, intimately.

Perfect*shun*ism causes us to fear the raw, unrefined inner experience and to shun what our souls are really crying out for. So we mask our imperfect pain with excessive activity, noise, programs, addictions, and the like. We may fear the brokenness of others, as well. If we run away from our own pain, shame, and brokenness, we will most likely run away from broken people who come to us in their time of need and desperation.

Perfect*shun*ism causes us to look like something we are not, which puts a barrier between who we really are and other people. It keeps us from "being." Since we will never be perfect, our attempts at showing people our perfection hides our inner selves from them. People then see and experience our personas, not the real us. If we relate to people and God as we think we should (like an actor), then we keep others from encountering the real us. Pretending keeps us from *being* and keeps others from truly *being* with us.

Who are we in our core? What is the essence of our being? How do we get out of the soul-sucking vortex of busyness, distractions, technological tethering, and perfectionistic tendencies? How do we avoid spiritual bypassing and find our authentic selves again? How do move from perfect-seeking human "doers" to content human "beings" who love God, self, and others with more gusto? Thankfully, in this book, Karl Forehand shows us a way.

Karl is a master storyteller. He also has the heart of a mystic and the mind of a brilliant archaeologist. His ability in this book to navigate the caverns of his experiences and extract timeless and liberating wisdom for us all will cause you to cry, laugh, be challenged, and simply be in awe. Most importantly, Karl will show you the path of "Being." Karl will show you how to be honest, brave, and authentic. He will show you how to be fully alive, fully you, and incredibly present—not just for your sake, but for the sake of others and ultimately the world. May you enjoy this gift as much as I did!

– **Mark Karris**

LICENSED THERAPIST AND BESTSELLING AUTHOR

INTRODUCTION

I learned the value of hard work from my family-of-origin early in life. Doing something was a way to be affirmed and rewarded. Even before my first paying job, my brother and I discovered we could scavenge for aluminum cans and sell them to a recycler. My mother encouraged us and even drove us to the recycling center, even though it likely cost more for the gas than we made.

Later we hauled buckets of manure to our huge, organic garden. I remember being very happy riding my bicycle several miles to pick okra for a farmer to both get out of laboring for my dad and to be paid in proportion to how hard I could work. I came to assume that working hard (doing) was the way to be rewarded.

But, even though I could work as hard or harder than my peers, I still felt disadvantaged. As a child, I had to wear thick glasses. I was short and skinny, but I worked hard and became the fullback on our high school football team. A few times, I fought with stockier guys to prove myself. In my younger years, our family struggled financially. That experience was also a motivation for me to work hard to find the financial and emotional rewards I felt I needed to have worth, value and security. It was much later that I realized this belief led me down an unhealthy path.

Too much of my drive was about accomplishment and *doing* at the cost of becoming. I did very well with the "you can do anything" mantra because I believed it. But it was never enough—I never hit the target, I never arrived at home and I never really found the peace my heart was seeking.

With marriage and then children, the whole *doing* thing got a lot more complicated for me. I discovered that I couldn't just work more or harder to make life work. My wife, our children, friends and then people in the churches I served expected different things from me. I found it simply wasn't enough just to perform.

Occasionally, I heard strange whispers, as if someone wandered by and softly said, "You are a human *being*, not a human *doing*." I would look around and wonder where the voice came from and then go back to my daily obligations. But the message kept creeping into my consciousness like a gentle breeze blowing through the trees.

As a pastor, I heard these whispers about this idea of *being* in Scripture. I read and wondered about Jesus' real meaning when he said to the disciples: "Come to me, all you that are weary and are carrying heavy burdens, and I will give you rest. Take my yoke upon you, and learn from me; for I am gentle and humble in heart, and you will find rest for your souls. For my yoke is easy, and my burden is light." This caused me to pause, but the *doing* of life jumped back into the driver's seat and I continued down the path that I was on.

Have you noticed that pastors like to talk about James' caution to be a "doers of the word and not just hearers?" Paul stressed that we are *servants* (doers) of Christ. I liked preaching about these things, because I learned that some Christians enjoy an occasional guilt trip, and I could mention the sign-up sheet for the nursery right after preaching about *doing* something instead of just hearing it. It was effective for people like me who got our self-worth from what we did. Something in me knew that this was just not *good news* for me or for anyone else but I would go back to more doing because it is what I knew best.

Something in me interpreted *being* as a copout. My usual strategy was running, searching and striving. I loved adventure, so my *doing* was always looking for a new strategy, the next "big thing" that would make up for my deficiencies and get me past the next hurdle.

After years of searching for worth, value and security through doing enough, I am now discovering a new way of being and becoming. I call it a *journey toward presence and authenticity.* Or if you like, *being where you are* and *being who you are*. It is not a static destination; it is an ongoing process—a meaningful and mysterious adventure.

I want you to know this being and becoming I have discovered. That is why I am writing this book. You may experience this book as one of those "whispers" in the midst of your life of doing. You may also consider my story as a guide for your journey toward authenticity and presence.

As we engage in sharing that journey together, some prep work is in order. If you are anything like me, you want to get started immediately building the structure. It is important to remember that restoring the foundation is important and sometimes walls must be torn down before we can remodel the house.

As you will see in my story, there can be devastating consequences when we rush forward with re-engineering our lives or our practices when we do not look below the surface.

Most of us have some past trauma and experiences that have created "emotional stoppages" that prevent us from *being* who we could be. That is why I begin this book with some of my history.

Part I is an accounting of probably the most significant event in my life. It wasn't my wedding day—it wasn't the birth of my children (although both of those are significant). It was a crisis. My friend, Dr. Paul Fitzgerald says, "Never waste a good crisis." This was a time where I felt like my life was over. It was one of the few times I considered taking my own life. This part reveals the hard work it took to come out of the crisis.

Part II was encouraged by another friend, Mark Karris, as I wrote the first part of this book. He encouraged me to dive deeper into some of my story and investigate some of these areas that are common to most people. We can continue to grow and heal and improve if we have the courage to dive deeper and find those parts of us that are wounded. I invite you along with me on this journey of discovery in some of these more common areas of struggle.

When we are willing to do the hard work of going deeper, we give ourselves the very real possibility to live vibrant and authentic lives. And that is Part III. But, please don't skip ahead!

I wish I could transport you to your new destination automatically. I wish I could magically make all your issues go away. I can't do that because it doesn't work that way. What I can do is walk with you on the journey as I invite you to gain courage and understanding from my story.

As I said in my previous book, *Apparent Faith*, "Let us walk together, you and I … and in doing so find peace!

Note: If you are going to any type of work that involves "going deeper," I would encourage you to enlist a trained counselor or a spiritual director. A companion is essential for the journey for many reasons.

PART I

Don't Waste a Good Crisis

WHAT IS HAPPENING?

> *"Never waste a good crisis."*
> DR. PAUL FITZGERALD

Have you ever driven somewhere and forgotten how you got there or just sat and stared and wondered "How long have I been here?" That was the kind of feeling that came over me about a half mile from our house. I was on our regular walking path, but I didn't remember how I got there. I do remember what I was muttering to myself, "I just can't believe it, I just can't believe it." Everything else seemed like a dream or memory that never really happened.

I don't know what I looked like and I really didn't care. I could feel my heart beating through my chest. My head was spinning in that kind of way that thoughts don't really run together or form coherent streams. The sensation I had was that my thoughts and imaginations were crashing into each other. Everything seemed like I was in a war. It was after a complete lap around the track that I heard the buzz of a text message.

When I saw Laura's text, it resonated as something she would normally say, but it didn't stop me from reacting. I was in full defense mode and my senses were on high alert. When she asked, "Are you okay?" I responded quickly and harshly like a small animal caught in a trap. I wasn't okay. I was about the furthest thing from being okay, and unfortunately my mind believed that it was her fault. I said, "I feel like you are abusing me." It felt good to say because it was how I felt.

I often wonder if people at war feel things like this. Do they pause in the middle of battle and think, "Wait, what am I doing here?" My partner of 29 years was on the other side of the battle, and to make it worse, her sister was visiting. In my mind, I was sure she was in on it. "She doesn't want us to be happy" is just one of the wild assumptions I made in the heat of the conflict. War requires you to be suspicious of everyone.

Her almost immediate response to my unusual accusation was, "Then why do you stay with me?" Soon after, I went into a tailspin and I don't remember anything I said after that. I'm not sure how long I walked or even physically coming back in the house. I was angry and confused, but mostly what I experienced was pain.

The pain that I felt that day was the deepest anguish I have ever felt in my life. It was the culmination of everything I have ever subdued in my psyche coming to the surface at one time. At least, that was my experience. But the path it took was not through normal channels. It went directly through my heart. I have never had a heart event like my father and grandfather, but this was what I imagine one would be like. My heart ached in ways I would have never thought possible. The dam was breaking, and I was like a little boy trying to plug the holes. The pressure was too great, and I finally passed out from exhaustion. My body literally couldn't take it anymore.

I woke up some time later that night when Laura asked me if I wanted to talk. I was coherent enough to know this may be the end of my marriage, so I spoke carefully. Digging deeper would come later, but neither one of us had the energy for that. It would be some time later before the defenses came down, but at least we were talking across the wall.

I had a lot of work to do and it wasn't going to be fun or easy and it didn't have six easy steps. I was about to begin a journey that I didn't want to go on. My mind frantically searched for an easy answer or quick fix and came up empty.

I fell back asleep sometime later. I slept hard, but this night's rest didn't resolve anything for me. My body physically felt like it did when we had two-a-day practices in football. I was rested but was physically sore even though I had done little physically to feel that way. This was too big to shove back inside. I was going to have to deal with it and I had no idea how.

THE WEEKEND

The weekend started out normal. We were planning to have a Hawaiian party with several of our friends. This rarely ever happens. Our youngest daughter left home a few years ago and while our children were around, we never really had people over. We weren't uptight or hard to get along with, we just never really had time to entertain. Being in the ministry meant, to some extent, that we were always the new people in town. We had dinner with some people early on, but then we weren't their best friends or their family, so normally we didn't have parties and we didn't get invited to a lot of them. Not to mention, all the normal stigmas that go along with hanging out with the pastor.

This party was going to be rather good. I have had several gatherings since leaving the ministry and I always served plant-based food because I love feeding people and I love convincing them that they can eat healthy and still enjoy it. This time was not different, our friends Paul and Susanna showed up early. We did a podcast and they watched me make the food for the evening. I remember making the fajitas and the quesadillas. Everything was shaping up for a good time. Even the people that were coming were a blessing.

Laura's sister was visiting. Contrary to popular belief, I love my mother-in-law and both of Laura's sisters. I think they are all wise, brave women. I always enjoy being around them. I say that because a later part of the story may have you wondering, but trust me, I'm always happy to see them and I think they are great. This sister, Karen, is fun to be around. She is in the medical field and has lots of fun stories. She also just has a pleasant nature about her, and I consider her to be quite wise. She is currently not married and was considering dating using some dating apps—that's important to the story.

The rest of the guests were a collection of people that we are close with. One of the people was in a spiritual formation group that I was associated with and she and her husband attended the church we went to at the time. The pastor from across the street also came. We enjoyed talking to her and she had attended a couple of our gatherings. We had some vegan friends that we begged to come because we like them so much. I recently interviewed them on my podcast as "some of my favorite vegans." There was really a wide variety of people of different ages, some were drinkers, and some were not. The non-drinkers took off a little early and there were only a few left when things got a little interesting.

This is how one of the worst weeks of my life began.

Laura and her sister and one of our favorite vegans were having a good time. They had been drinking a little more than the rest of the crowd and then moved the party out to the porch and were basically having a good ole time. Normally, Laura would be telling me to hold it down, but this night the shoe was on the other foot. It was kind of an obnoxious version of them finding their voice.

They probably needed this release, and I wasn't trying to make them do anything. We were a little concerned about being in a small town that people would get upset if we were too loud. I wanted them to have a good time, just not at my expense and it felt like it was moving that way.

The next part I remember was the dating app. Laura's sister had been talking about going out with a guy in our area. I have always hoped that she would find the right guy. I don't know how to tell her how to find the right guy because I haven't dated in over 30 years. But the next chapter of the story starts with the dating app, where apparently you can scroll through potential matches and then based on your interests, make choices to pursue or not.

I was sitting in my chair when I noticed Laura's sister was showing her some of the potential candidates. Pretty normal thing for two sisters to do, I guess. Karen was saying, "see this one" and "what about this one" as she scrolled through the online pictures. You know how one of those feelings grows within you. Suddenly, I felt pressure and I thought, "Why is Laura looking at pictures of guys" and suddenly my mind was racing with all kinds of thoughts. I got up and walked around through the other side of the house and took another glance at them and disappeared into my bedroom.

I began to wonder "Is that what she really wants?' I think I asked about it later and she said she wasn't even looking at it. My mind was reacting to something and it wasn't a dating app. It also wasn't really my wife, Laura. People usually call my wife "a gem" or "a treasure." She does have a few flaws, but to me, those are the endearing qualities about her. She loves people and stands up for the little ones in her classroom. She is literally one of the best people I have ever met, and I love her deeply. So why was I acting, or better yet, reacting in this way?

The next clue was the plant-based event we went to the next day. The group which we had volunteered for in the past was having an event to serve some of their vegan food to people that wanted to come and try something different. We had done many of these events. Laura liked going with me, but this was before she found her voice. She never really said she didn't like going, but she just went because she knew I wanted to go. When she said she didn't want to go that day, I thought she was just being difficult. I don't even want to tell you some of the things that were running through my head. Regardless, she and her sister came along.

We served vegan sausage and burgers as people came up to visit. I say we, but what I really mean was me. Laura and her sister mostly sat under the tent and talked about how much fun they were not having. Probably not her best day, but at most she was being a little childish. I thought, "Why are you here if you don't really want to be here—what good does it do to come and then just complain?" Remember that thought. Eventually I would evolve this theology to where I believed she was just trying to abuse me.

Somehow on the ride home, I interpreted more of her actions to be a part of this plan that she supposedly had. It sounded to me like they were going to get back at me for dragging them on this trip, so I thought I heard her order me to ride in the back seat on the way home. It wasn't a discussion—more like a command. I don't think I'm the controlling type, but since I was reading this into everything that happened, I continued on the theme as before—she must be trying to whatever—embarrass me, control me, or just torture me.

But this time, I was silent in the back seat. Then it happened again. Karen showed Laura another person on the dating app, and Laura swerved a little. I don't remember anything that I thought from that point on except my mind was playing a movie I couldn't stop. Why was she doing this? What did I do wrong? I just can't believe it—this may be the end!

Those were the thoughts racing through my mind as I stumbled out onto our home sidewalk and eventually found myself a half mile away trying to make sense of what was happening. Looking back, I have no reason to say this; but, at the time, I asked "Why is she doing this?"

It would be much later in the story before I realized that I was not thinking straight, but this issue that I'm talking about didn't start in 2018. It started way back probably before I even remember.

MY HISTORY WITH REJECTION

"As our conditioning establishes itself in us, it so dominates our psychological and emotional landscape that we normalize it."
ROBERT AUGUSTUS MASTERS[1]

My wife thinks a lot about abandonment. Her parents are divorced, but then her father also left all his daughters without any explanation. So, while I find it hard to relate to, she very much thinks a lot about whether people are going to leave her. Many of the women that befriended her while I was a pastor, abandoned her just as quickly when things didn't go their way. Her biggest complaint about church and ministry is the women that didn't follow through on their friendships and left her without warning.

My story is less about abandonment and more about rejection. There are many reasons a person might leave or abandon another, and they are usually not rejecting them. Nobody abandoned me necessarily, but I still felt rejected.

I remember an intense scene from my childhood. My mother confirmed the story a few years ago. I was feeling underappreciated for whatever reason. I was the oldest of five children but also a little timid and unsure of myself. We lived in a tiny house where I remember my youngest brother sleeping at the foot of my sister's bed. It would take too long to explain, but suffice to say, we were like sardines in this

---

[1] Masters, Robert Augustus, *Bringing Your Shadow Out of the Dark: Breaking Free from the Hidden Forces That Drive You*, Boulder, CO: Sounds True, 2018

house. And, as always with five children, it's hard to get much individual attention or preferential treatment.

I don't remember specifically what happened that day, but I blurted out to one of my younger brothers, "Mom likes Karla (my sister) and dad likes Monty (a brother) and no one likes us." I'm sure my mom reassured me, but we really didn't talk about things like that at length. There just wasn't much time in a house with five kids. Just like my wife, my mom did an outstanding job raising us. I still consider her to be one of the strongest women I know, but the circumstances of our life were not ideal, and we just never really talked about our feelings or things like that. I remember hearing that life wasn't fair, but I didn't know what to do about it.

Around the age of five, I was fitted for glasses. But mine were not the cute kind like my grandson, Jackson, got. No, my glasses were what would affectionately be termed "coke bottles" by people in my life. My glasses are a part of me, but I always felt they automatically classified me also. I assumed my glasses gave the impression I was smart, not athletic and not quite as cool as the other kids. I would say this was the beginning of my drive to fit in. Add to this that I was smaller than most of the boys and my clothes weren't always the latest fashion. I just always felt like I was working from a deficit. So, I tried harder and did what I could and what I felt like I needed to fit in.

The only fights I got into growing up were with bullies. I think I still have a strong aversion to people that are naturally bigger, stronger, and faster that use their privilege to push other people down. Because I had a deep need to fit in, the people that tried to stop me from fitting in were the enemy. I know now that they were navigating their own struggles and dysfunctional families. All of us humans seem to have a deep desire to fit into community but making that happen is usually quite messy and complicated. I often concluded that I was on the outside, living on the fringes, trying to get into something. Even though I have had the privilege of being a white male, it never felt like much of an advantage to me.

I suppose the opposite sex have always been a part of this challenge. I'm still not totally comfortable around them. I want to be respectful and charming, but it seems like there are too many things I should and shouldn't say and I forget to be authentic. I'm glad that Laura was forgiving when I met her, because I said the wrong thing the first time we met. Somehow, she let me into the inner circle, and we have navigated about three decades even though I still get tongue-tied around her.

I was probably around 14 or 15 when we started looking at Charlies Angels pictures in the bathroom. This is the first I remember of being attracted to the opposite sex except for that one girl in second grade. It wasn't long before everyone wanted to have a girlfriend, whatever that meant at that time. If you add to the mix the beginnings of the Purity Culture, you can probably imagine this was a pretty dysfunctional time for me. Loads of shame were heaped on anything sexual or passionate. Even though it seemed like this terribly important subject, not a word was spoken about it. We didn't even talk about how to treat a woman or have a healthy relationship. All those topics were off the table because they didn't want us thinking about sex—especially at a Christian school.

My first heartbreak was in Junior high. I came back from being on vacation to find one of my best friends sitting next to my "girlfriend" at the basketball game. When I say, "she was my girlfriend," what I mean is that I probably sent her a note saying, "I like you—do you like me? Check Yes or No." It's the way you did things in Jr. High. If she said, "yes" then I was accepted, and we could sit together at church activities and sporting events. We were going steady. None of us spoke about the rejection, we just continued through our Junior High lives.

I don't know about you, but situations like this left me wondering *why*. "Why did she choose the other guy instead of me? I'll bet it was the glasses—someday I'll get contacts. Maybe I just need to get stronger or faster or smarter." Since we don't really have the capacity to process all that and adults don't seem to be interested in talking about it, we usually submerge those questions and concerns and move on with our lives and focus our attention on being accepted by the new girl that has bigger boobs anyway.

I know the tendency to dismiss these kinds of thoughts and experiences as normal is common. It must be common because another one of my friends stole my girlfriend in high school. We had gone to the prom together and I was looking forward to pursuing the relationship only to find out she had caught the attention of, literally, my best friend. I'm not sure how he and I stayed friends, but I didn't do so well coping with the situation. I remember crying—not just tears, but a deep, sobbing type of crying—in my room in the basement. It must have been noticeable because my dad came down to check on me. He didn't really have the skills to counsel me, but he did his best to console me, at least enough to stuff that pain down and continue with my quest to fit in. I didn't really have any significant relationships in high school, even though I thought about girls all the time.

Football was another one of my pursuits. I started playing football in the 3rd grade, so I already had some good and bad habits. Our coach, in this tiny town, was an ex-professional football player. He was very smart but talked in a very slow Oklahoma drawl. We didn't really have to make the team because we barely had enough players to field a team. That said, the coach had me scoped out as a fullback, but because there was a super big, fullback looking guy on the team I got to sit on the bench for the first half of my sophomore season. This seemed to be the norm for me. I was faster and smarter than this guy, but I didn't look like someone that could do the job. This is a great example of how I lived most of my life, trying to convince people to "put me in the game." When the lead runner went down with an injury, I became the starting fullback and made sure I proved them wrong. I was all-conference my senior year and established a pattern I would repeat the rest of my life. I felt if I could just get my foot in the door, I could work harder and outsmart just about anyone with my determination.

Even now past 50 years old, I still feel like people misjudge me. Is that a vibe I'm putting out or is it just what people do? Just like the football situation, I can name only a few times in my life where I was picked for the team. I hear potential employers say, "We didn't think you'd be interested" or "this probably isn't something for you." I continually keep reminding people that I'm interested. You know how when you go to a baseball game and invite a friend along? I have literally never been invited to a concert or a baseball game or anything like that, except for a few things that were ministry related or I was already on the team. People just assume that I wouldn't be interested or maybe they just don't think I would be whatever they are desiring for that event. Even when I was a pastor, I experienced feeling rejected.

So, my strategy for many years has been to work hard at fitting in. I hear you saying, that's not the best idea, but a couple of church planters encouraged me to keep doing it. They said the best way to build a church is to go out and do what people are doing, go to their sporting events, root for their teams, and become like them. This was almost second nature for me, and I was pretty good at it. All three churches I pastored grew and flourished for a time, until I started to be a little more authentic and then things leveled off.

They all liked me when I left because when they liked golf, I played golf. When there were hunters in the crowd, I learned to hunt. When they cheered for the Nebraska Cornhuskers, I still cheered for Oklahoma (my hypocrisy only goes so far). It's a fine line sometimes between being relatable and the falseness of trying desperately to fit it. But I was way across the line and eventually I came to a point where I couldn't do it anymore.

One of the revelations I am discovering is that this practice I had of trying to fit in only made me more invisible. When I made myself just like the people around me, it only made them disregard me even more. They accepted me as one of their own, part of their body, but usually we don't think about the individual parts of our body—we just take it for granted! And that's where I would usually end up in my job, the churches and my personal life. Trying to fit in and then trying to stand out. It's a hard game to play with little rewards and lots of pain. Rejection seemed so much more personal because of how hard I had to work to be accepted.

These are some of the things that led up to my breakdown that Sunday afternoon.

More than anyone else in the world, I wanted to be accepted by my wife. I avoid the term "my best friend," because she is so much more than that. As I have said many times, she is literally the best person I know. I can't imagine life without her. We have been through so many things together including ministry, raising children, and moving around the country. We have started over several times including when we started in ministry and then when we left it. I feel like I can do anything with her, but I can't imagine thriving without her in my life.

So, what happened that weekend? Was she rejecting me or was I repeating a pattern that had been played out most of my life? As difficult situations happened in my life, I repeatedly did the minimum I had to so that I could continue with life. It seemed like a way to survive. I had to go back to work, I had to do ministry and we had to get back to raising our children. In a way, I was repeating the pattern of my parents. When I realized my time and resources were limited, I went back to work, got back in the game, and went on about my business doing the best I could to forget about the things I didn't really understand.

But this weekend seemed like something bigger. Or, maybe my collection of things that I was stuffing down would no longer fit in the place where I kept them? Maybe the work I had been doing in spiritual formation and with a community called Heart Connexion was opening me up to something? I had no idea about any of it except that my primary thought was that Laura was rejecting me even though it made no sense at all.

I went to bed on Sunday night and did my best to tuck all the edges in so that I could get up on Monday morning and go back to my new job and get past this thing—whatever it was. This plan never had a chance of working, but I didn't know what else to do!

GOING BACK TO WORK

> *"Though we may think we're done with our past, our past isn't necessarily done with us—and it won't be until we recognize its impact on us and begin the work of not letting ourselves be run by it, of bringing it out of our shadow."*
> ROBERT AUGUSTUS MASTERS

My very first job was working in my father's garden. For a time, my parents were organic gardeners and they raised worms. Those two things kind of worked together. It's one the hobbies my family had that worked out well. We lived in that tiny house, but we had lots of vegetables and plenty to sell. Early on I desired to have money of my own, even though I usually just spent it on food or pop or baseball caps. My first job I can remember is picking up aluminum cans. We would walk the highway near our house and bring back loads of cans so my mom could take us to redeem them later.

My first real job was probably around age 13 or 14. We worked for a farmer that grew lots of okra and different varieties of peppers. To harvest the okra, we had to wear long sleeves and those gloves that you wear to wash dishes. Once we were deemed capable enough, we got to pick peppers. We also had to wear gloves to harvest the peppers, but we also had to be careful not to step on them toward the middle of the day when it was hot. It was a hard job for a 14 year old, but I remember riding our bicycles about 3 miles very early in the morning to get the chance to make some money that we usually spent on the way home at the convenience store. I remember the lunch meat sandwiches he used to serve us, and I remember what he used to say.

He said, "When I come by the field, I want to see A's and E's—asses and elbows." It meant that he wanted our heads down and us working every moment. I learned how I should work from people like this.

My next real job was when we moved to Lone Wolf, OK. I was there a few months when I got a job on a harvest crew. I would get to drive a combine for about $3 per hour. I went to tractor driving school (yeah, it's a real thing) and began the summer learning to use tools and work on the equipment. The job driving a combine was easy, but sometimes dirty and very long hours. The job ended early though when the whole crew got drunk and made some errors in judgement. I was too young to really be involved, but I was retained to help drive some of the equipment home before I even had a driver's license.

I generally like working and that was what I was thinking on this Monday morning after the weekend. I reasoned that maybe if I can just get back to work and get in my routine, this whole thing would straighten itself out. As I was driving the hour drive to work at an Ethanol plant, I couldn't help but notice that this felt different. There was more residual pain than the times before. There was kind of a dull ache that wasn't going away. I was trying to remember what I had to do at work, but I couldn't remember anything. The closer I got to work the more I realized that this was going to be difficult.

I sought out my boss to tell him I was having problems. He was very understanding. I went back up to my desk and I just cried a few times before I did anything. I asked to be dismissed from the morning meeting which was tough to sit through without being in my current condition. While the others were having a meeting outside my office, I was trying to find a place to stay for a few days. I wasn't thinking about leaving Laura, but I knew I had to get away for at least a few days. I needed some distance.

A few months prior I started into a spiritual formation program called Souljourners. It was orchestrated by the Benedictine Sisters in Atchison, KS. Several of my friends from different places were participating or had participated in this program that produces Spiritual Directors. Spiritual Directors are like counselors, but with a much more contemplative bent. They were extremely good at listening and helping people access what is inside. In retrospect, I know that my sessions with that group and with my spiritual director, Sister Marcia, was opening me up and beginning to discover what many might call the shadow part of me.

We were due to have the next overnight session in about four days, so I made a desperate call to ask them if I could stay in the hermitage there on campus until it was time for our normal sessions on Friday. They agreed and I began to prepare to leave immediately. I couldn't work, I couldn't go home, and I couldn't think straight. So, I headed to Atchison. Even though I was leaving home for now, something in me felt like I was coming home to myself.

LEAVING HOME

Another thing that had happened recently was my participation in an experience called BreakThrough. It is an immersive experience that deals with many issues. Soon after, I had traveled to Taiwan to see my son and had the Tea Shop experience. I talked about these experiences in my previous books, *Apparent Faith* and *The Tea Shop*. Both experiences helped me grow and deal with the shame of my past. I was growing every day, but like layers of an onion, new things were being exposed. It was kind of like the façade of my house had been pulled back and now I didn't want to face what I saw there. I wanted to ignore it or blame it on Laura. So, I left and went to Atchison, but it followed me there.

I texted Laura on the way there. I basically just told her that I needed to get away. She admitted later that she didn't know for sure if I was coming back. She was accustomed to the perception and experience of people leaving her. Knowing this, her mind was probably producing the scenario of abandonment the same way I struggle with rejection. She knew this was different from all the other times when we had a little spat. This experience was different and both of us recognized that. The trouble was that we had never walked this path before. We were in desperate need of help, but at that moment, we couldn't help each other.

I also talked to Sister Marcia on the way there. She is literally one of the most "tuned-in" people I know of spirituality. I set an appointment with her later that day, I was desperate, and she agreed to meet me to see if we could make some progress. I checked into the Hermitage and sat down and wrote down my thoughts. The gist of what I was saying to myself was still focused on blaming Laura and pity for myself. I remember writing, "I just don't understand why she is doing this? Why am I having to go through this? Why am I not better than this?" It was a full-blown, raging pity party and I was the only one invited. Maybe it was a shame shitstorm, I don't know. Nothing made much sense at all, and I couldn't label anything.

Contemplative Companions, as they are referred to, are a little different than a counselor. They don't really like to be called directors, because they don't usually "direct" anything or give advice. They usually have a lot of wisdom, but they allow you to discover your wisdom yourself. They just like to help you along as you journey toward discovering sometimes what you already know. What I should have known that day was that Laura didn't really do anything to provoke me. Her actions were normal, and I was the one that was reacting to everything.

While Sister Marcia doesn't usually give advice, she had something to say to me that afternoon. I know I'm probably misquoting her, but she said something along these lines. She said, "You know Laura wasn't doing anything wrong," and then she looked at me. Oh my, I can't begin to tell you what kind of shift started taking place in that moment! I believe she went on to say that basically I need to make the most of my time in the Hermitage and go inside to find the answers to this. We talked for nearly an hour, but I can't remember anything except I know she cared about me and I wanted to get to the bottom of this. We discussed shadow and how you could "make friends" with those parts of you. I didn't begin to understand what that meant but I was genuinely curious.

Earlier I had talked to my friend Dr. Paul Fitzgerald. He is also a spiritual director and shame expert and has led thousands of people to live better lives because of the work he and his wife Susanna do. I am lucky to have him as a friend. He casually mentioned, "Maybe it's time you do some shadow work." He recommended a book by Robert Augustus Masters called *Bringing Your Shadow out of the Dark*. I checked the book out from Kindle, but I didn't start reading it until in the morning. I went and got some food, fixed myself dinner and settled in for the night.

My faith tradition taught me a kind of spiritual laziness. I was taught to pray for things and they would magically be solved. I wasn't taught that challenging life experiences would take work, but I was about to find out exactly what was involved. I was about to do some of the hardest work I had ever done in my life, including picking okra. I had a good solid meal that night. That was good because it was going to be a while before I would eat again.

I texted Laura, but I was still raw, so I basically let her know that I was okay. I can only imagine what she was thinking. Remember she has a predisposition to believe that people tend to leave her. As I write this, I am at a month-long training seminar and I can't afford to fly home. I know it's hard for her, but both of us are better off right now than we were. I knew that just being gone was going to take some repair and reconciliation; but I also knew that unless I got alone, I wasn't going to get through what I needed to get through.

I fell asleep almost instantly, not because there was nothing on my mind, but because I was once again exhausted.

IT ALL HAPPENED IN A RECLINER

The next morning, I was awake way before dawn, and I started reading the book *Bringing Your Shadow Out of the* Dark by Robert August Masters. It wasn't the kind of reading where you read until your mind wanders a little and then put it down—then pick it back up and fall asleep. This was what I would call fully engaged reading! I was reading every single word, underlining about half of it, then after every chapter, I would type the notes into a laptop. This felt very urgent to me, but I didn't know exactly why.

I think I was just that determined to get this right. If two people on the same day recommended the same topic, I was going to study the life of that subject. And I had no other options. No one else was offering any good advice. Many of the strategies in my life had failed. I had many things going for me, but this recurring issue had plagued me my whole life. I had gained ground in other training, but my hope was this shadow work might be the answer.

Masters' book was new, and I wanted to hear exactly what he had to say. I had to at least try. I certainly didn't have any more to lose. My marriage was in trouble. I couldn't go back to work. I told myself, *with all the work I had done in the past, I'll be damned if I'm going to die on this hill.* I can't afford to give up, but I don't have a clue what to do.

What I Was Learning From Robert Masters

Early in the book, Masters gives a concise definition of shadow that got me started on the right path.

> Our shadow is the place within each of us that contains what we do not know, don't like or deny about ourselves ... Our shadow holds our unattended and not-yet-illuminated conditioning—all the programmed ways we act, think, feel and choose without knowing why.[2]

That was exactly what I was feeling. Even with all the work I had done over the years there were still things inside me that I didn't fully understand or like so much. These were the things that kept getting pushed back down inside there. The trouble was that they didn't stay there. They occasionally came out sideways and it seemed to be getting worse. In fact, Masters stated something like this when he said, "the more we push it away or ignore it, the stronger and more rooted it becomes, insinuating its way into our everyday life."

I don't know if you've ever watched a documentary or read a sacred text or heard a poem or read a book that truly nailed your situation. It was almost like I stopped breathing for a second. I not only understood what he was saying, but I was living out the experience in my life. I had used almost every strategy and technique to maneuver around my shadow. The times that I had gotten close to it, I used spiritual bypassing or charm or excuses to move past. But the shadow didn't go away, it didn't get better and I still had the issue that recurred.

Another thing that I could not deny from the book is that *reactivity* was a huge part of this issue, especially in that it was involved in most of my encounters with my shadow. In fact, the whole weekend in question was my reaction and overreaction to simple things that

---

2   Masters, Robert Augustus, *Bringing Your Shadow Out of the Dark: Breaking Free from the Hidden Forces That Drive You*, Boulder, CO: Sounds True, 2018

normally wouldn't have even caught my attention, much less caused me to react that way that I did.

Now that I am aware of it, I see it every day. There was the guy that didn't get his way in a hardware store and threw all his merchandise in the street and demanded a refund. Another person cussed out the waiter and made them feel like dirt because their food wasn't exactly right. When I get unusually upset at someone on Facebook because they dared to contradict me. All of us have experienced situations like this.

Perhaps, shadow is also connected to *fear*. Masters explains how fear doesn't have to be a bad thing. He challenged me to "get to know my fear." That is an interesting supposition. I know Christianity teaches us not to fear, but then almost every Christian I know seems to be dominated by fear. We often use that fear to control situations and other people, so we won't be afraid anymore—but it doesn't work. It helps to imagine that maybe there is some type of inner child that still affects us and still causes us to react and over-react. I wanted to understand this fear that was rooted inside me.

Another big subject of the book was *anger*. For many of us, we were discouraged from being angry. We intellectually knew anger wasn't "a sin." But we were all too cautious not to outwardly express the anger that we might have felt inside. Again, Masters warns of the danger "By keeping our anger in our shadow—muzzled, locked up, chained—and denying it any care and light, we only increase the odds that it will misbehave when it breaks out." What we often say about other people, we could say about this part of us that wants to behave wrongly. It just needs compassion and love—it really needs grace and mercy—it really needs a hug.

There are so many lessons I was learning. So much of this book was resonating with me. I don't know how many times I said, "Oh, wow!" and then just sat there for 10 or 15 minutes. And then, I dived back into another topic, only to pause and think about how this made perfect sense. But even my heightened level of focus was yearning for something tangible that I could do. Thankfully, the answers to a way forward started to reveal themselves. But, before I tell you that, let me share some guidelines that might help your journey. It certainly has mine.

Some Guidelines

It has become helpful over the past few years to understand the simple fact that we are on a lifelong *journey*. It helps me so much to call my story a journey or adventure, because then I don't have to write the ending yet. I don't have to have all the answers—I don't have to solve all my problems. I just must stay on the road and even occasionally wander off it.

I am also learning that when I go down a road that I have never been down, then it is probably going to seem unfamiliar to me—because it is. I could never have imagined what I was embarking upon. But I didn't progress on the journey by mapping it out. I had to take the *courageous steps* I knew to take and keep my eyes open for clues to the next step of faith. We talk about faith but then we revert to what we already know which has only taken us where we've already been. That usually doesn't help us all that much, especially with things like shadow. In fact, often it just bypasses it and causes it to get worse.

The fear that the things like shadow work would lead me down some type of *dark alley* often kept me stuck where I was. I used spiritual bypassing to spiritualize my fear and stop me from trying something that people in the church might not have known so much about. Then, I could either hide either in my communities or away from them, instead of facing the things I needed to.

Shame and past regrets also supposed that being vulnerable was just too big of a risk because I had been hurt before. In a way, I used my reactionary response as motivation and I said things like "I can't do this anymore" and "I have to get to the bottom of this" so even if it is a dark alley, I'm hoping there's a light at the other end. I didn't know what else to do.

I was still sitting in the recliner when I read about my inner child and how I should be present with my hurt. I have since learned also that the goal is not to eradicate anything but to bring it into my awareness and have compassion for it. A common term used by Masters and others is to "hold space" for our shadow. An experienced spiritual director can lead a person in a focusing session to see exactly where we are holding things in our body. Masters talks about a similar practice in his book. When we're ready and willing these things can be brought to the surface.

I'm pretty sure I didn't do everything right or even understand it, but this is what happened to me that day. Take a deep breath and then make sure and let it out!

What Happened Next

The book told me to place my hands onto the place where I felt upset. My spiritual director tells me something similar. I placed my hand on my heart because it had been aching for days now. Ever since this thing started my heart had felt a heaviness and a sadness as severe as anything I had ever experienced. We talk about our hearts metaphorically, but this was as much physical as it was emotional or spiritual. I could feel it almost as though my heart was trying to push its way outside my chest. There was real pressure—there was real pain—there was real emotion.

As I put my right hand over my chest, I could feel my heart beating strong within my palm. As I considered the following words, it seemed to beat slower and much stronger almost as if time was slowing down. I could feel it beating inside my temples. I wasn't panicking and I wasn't even afraid. As I read these words from Robert August Masters, I simply felt a strong confidence and then something else I had not ever felt before. This is what I read out loud from the book, but I don't think the actual words are what is important. I said:

> "I see you. I understand why you feel this way, and I've got your back. I'll take care of you, and I'll take care of what is happening."

Immediately I began to weep in a different way than I ever had. It was more of a groaning where I felt like in a way, like I was being reborn. I would say it was like a heart attack, but It wasn't that kind of pain. It was like something was coming out but not really leaving me. Instantly I started thinking about each of my children and grandchildren and future grandchildren. I thought back over parts of my childhood and literally could sense a younger version of myself.

Every time that my children, grandchildren or my younger self came to mind, I said, "I got your back." What I meant was that I see you,

I hear you, I love you and I don't want you to be afraid anymore. I meant that I know part of me tends to be critical of other parts of myself. I understood that I had to help parts of myself that were captive to my thinking that I was protecting them when I was really kind of torturing them. I had to bring all that shadow out of the dark and let them know "I got your back."

Although I didn't know what most of that meant, I felt a peace greater than what I felt lately. Much of the anxiety went away instantly. My body felt like falling asleep, but my soul felt alive. I suddenly realized how long it had been since I had eaten and so I walked over and fixed a simple meal without saying a word. As I would take a bite, I would occasionally be compelled to return to the place I had just been, and I would cry out (in anguish? In joy?)! I didn't see revelations of God or the Beatles or anything like that. But I did keep experiencing occasionally what I will never forget. It was joy, it was a good kind of pain, it was compassion, it was gratitude. It was many things—it was most definitely good.

As I stood between the inner critic and my inner child, I realized I had compassion for both of them. Other than that, I didn't realize anything else except that my life was going to be different and it certainly has been. I texted Dr. Paul throughout this ordeal, but I cannot remember what he said, or if my texts even made any sense. I fell asleep again that night easily, once again because I was exhausted.

TELLING MY STORY

I interviewed William Paul Young some time back on my podcast, the Desert Sanctuary. In my interview and others, I have heard him talking fondly about the sacredness of other people's stories. In a way, we are our stories and when we share them with others, we share a part of ourselves. I didn't know what I was supposed to do next, so I started reading the books I had with me, but I had a suspicion that the next thing I would do is to tell my story. I knew that this new awareness and experience that had happened in me needed to be shared.

The spiritual direction training was about to start in a day or two, so I knew I would have multiple opportunities to share over the weekend. I knew I needed to share with Laura, but there was too much pain still. I told her basically what was going on—that I was working with my spiritual directors and that it was going well. She didn't say much, but it sounded like she was trying to understand. I wanted to make it all better for her, but I couldn't manage two things at once. I was trying to do the hard work where I was, and I just prayed she could hang on a little longer. Not that I was going to necessarily make it all better for her, but I was certainly trying to make myself better so I would be better equipped to do my part in healing what was broken there.

I talked to Dr. Paul Fitzgerald and tried to explain what had happened so far. He gave me bits of direction like he does in just the right amount. I was happy to have him along and later I got to talk to Sister Marcia again. They were both very gently guiding me along and, in a way, the start of telling my story began with them. I just can't begin to tell you how well they were listening. If I could change one thing about the world, I would make us better listeners. I don't remember if they encouraged me to tell my story, but somehow, I knew it was the right thing to do.

By the time people started to arrive early on Friday, I had leaked to some of my close friends what was going on and they all wanted to hear my story. Each time I told my story and saw their eyes of grace, a little bit of the shame peeled off and I felt like I was headed in the right direction. They listened intently and, since they were all contemplative types, they listened well. Eventually they would thank me for sharing my story. Not one of them gave me any advice, they just thanked me for sharing my story, cried with me and then gave me a simple but appropriate embrace.

We had group sessions later where I was able to share some of that story again and work through some of the rough edges of what I was discovering. Telling my story was vital to my healing. It took some of the shame away and gave me confidence that I was thinking correctly. It also let me know that I was not alone. In very subtle ways, some of these ladies that participated in the spiritual direction training with me let know that they had gone through similar experiences. When they would look at me with empathy, I felt like I was not alone even though I was beginning to miss Laura so much.

I really cannot speak to other people's experiences, but when I told my story, it caused me to go back inside and remember what it was like to bring my shadow out of the dark. When I relived this, it reminded me that there's a false image I had been portraying to others. I wasn't living from my true story, but rather living from the one that my life was writing for me.

Telling my story reassured me that I'm not alone. There are others that share the same struggles. There are others that care about the struggles I have, even though it doesn't feel like it some days. When I can't tell my story and my life is not authentic enough to portray my true story, people have no idea what to do for me even if they are trained. I must speak from my heart before they can ever possibly know what would help me.

Telling my story also makes me *vulnerable*. In junior high, I had experiences where I shared something that made me vulnerable and most times it was met with shaming behavior. Adults usually don't mean to shame us, but they say things like "you shouldn't be struggling with that" or even our own minds convince us that people won't understand or they are going to just make it more painful for us to be open and vulnerable. But there is no real intimacy without vulnerability, and we must take a calculated risk with genuine people and share our story.

On Saturday afternoon, I went home to see Laura. I remember us talking and her agreeing to see a spiritual director, mainly for my sake. She was loving as always, but suspicious. It was almost like starting our marriage over again. In the months ahead, I would prove to her that a lot of the reactionary part of me was gone. Sometime later, I remember saying, "I really don't react like that anymore" or she would say "you really don't do that anymore." I was far from perfect, but I was learning to engage with my shadow self. At times I would notice I was making great progress and occasionally I would notice myself slipping. It is a journey and I'm still not perfect.

The most amazing thing to me is what happened when I touched base with the shadow or inner child in me. When I do that now, I get a sense in my body of what I felt on that Tuesday a couple of years ago. It could be when I'm inspired by music or I read something that resonates with that part of me. Or even sometimes when I'm just mindful or breathing well. I sort of make the same sound, even if it's under my breath. I feel the same sensation and it helps me navigate my life with more of a heart-felt sense of direction than the reactionary response to life I was so accustomed to.

Over time, as I told my story and made space for this other part of me, I felt like my authentic self was emerging. I couldn't bear any more to just react to life, and I was beginning to live with a deep connection to the part of me that I knew was attached to the divine. It all began with telling a few people, from deep in my heart, just exactly what I went through one Tuesday afternoon.

That is what I do with my books, blogs and podcasts. I just keep telling my story. If the divine is in us, then the primary way that we commune together is through our stories. I hope to keep telling my story for as a long as I can. I know that it's not all written. But I know it's going to be good!

Now let's go a little deeper.

PART II

Going Deeper

GOING DEEPER WITH MY FEAR

My parents told stories about me as a young child. They said that when people would come to our house, I would hide under the coffee table. I do not remember everything that happened to me as a child, but I remember certain things. One day, walking home from school, some kids started yelling at us and teasing us. When one of the girls came up and stole my sister's glasses, I chased her down and made her give them back, but I remember shaking from all the adrenaline and it made me a little more fearful.

Soon after the glasses incident, I saw my first dog get run over and subsequently witnessed more bullying first-hand. I realized the world can be a bit of a dangerous place. Something inside me desperately wanted to overcome these fears. Later, I heard my grandfather talking about my dad. What he was actually doing was making fun of my dad for never learning how to swim. My grandfather was a pretty gentle man, but I assume this was just part of the way people sometimes hoped to motivate people out of their fearful actions with shame. I don't think it's very effective.

My grandfather's shaming words did influence me. I didn't want to be afraid like my dad. By that I mean that I didn't want to ever not try something because I was afraid. I didn't want to end up regretting portions of my life where I had opportunities and didn't experiment. So, experiment I did! I made 11 skydiving jumps, which is still one of the most exciting things I have ever done. I tried marijuana and alcohol and all the associated "vices" you could probably imagine. I learned karate up to a point, I mastered parts of hunting, I became proficient at golf—all just enough to get a sense of what it was like to be immersed in them, then I set them aside.

I never really had an intention of making those things into lifelong pursuits, I just wanted to know what it was like and I didn't want to miss out. I was a bit obsessive with all these pursuits because I wanted to know what it was like to be good at things. This challenge kept me interested and, I suppose, led me through whatever fear I had. I remember a couple of times like when I was fishing all night and when I was in a tree stand hunting deer and genuinely being terrified. Occasionally I would just leave and come home, but most of the time I persevered through the fear and found some sense of accomplishment in most endeavors.

I'm told fear is not necessarily bad. I suppose it gives us some warning signs of danger and if we take appropriate precautions, we can keep ourselves alive and safe. To live totally without any fear seems a little reckless and irresponsible. But, like many things, it can go beyond its natural limits. We can become over planners and always be on edge because of what might happen. Many of us use control, thinking it will alleviate our fear. It usually only makes it worse.

When I landed my first real job after Tech School, it was in Dallas, Texas. I remember going to the Human Resources office and walking past the tall buildings. I could see the cars up on the interstate and miles of congested traffic. The parking lots were full of cars and people seemed to be just streaming in and out of the building. My mind flashed back to Lone Wolf, Oklahoma which was my hometown. If two people were on main street at the same time, that was considered "busy." But standing in Dallas, Texas next to the large buildings, I felt small—I felt insignificant—I felt afraid.

My fears were not of doing things. I played football in high school even though I only weighed 150 pounds. My coach, Dale Meinert, instilled in us a fearlessness mainly because we were extremely frightened of him. Not because he would physically hurt us, but because like most coaches, he knew how to make you feel small when you weren't performing. It's a weird catch-22. We're trying to overcome one fear by submitting to another one. But after football and karate and skydiving and hunting in the woods, I wasn't physically afraid of much. My fears in these areas were somewhat reasonable.

When I was younger, I went by the name "*Joey*." My middle name is *Joseph* and my Grandpa Joe was called *Jody* or *Little Joe*. My first name is Karl and my grandpa were called *Karl Sr.* and my dad was called *Karl Jr.*, so I adopted the nickname *Joey* throughout my childhood. When I started to do shadow work, it seemed appropriate to use this name. It represented the little boy that hid under the coffee table because he was afraid of people. It was what I went by in college when I nearly flunked my speech class because I was so afraid of what people would think. Joey would eventually jump out of a perfectly good airplane to get a rush but could barely lead a silent prayer without passing out. This was what I learned about my fear—it was mainly a fear of people and what they would think about me. I needed approval—I needed to fit in—but I was so deathly afraid of what they might think, I often froze up and only reluctantly opened up to people.

I realized that over the years, I had nurtured a certain type of boldness and subdued courageousness in other areas. People were complicated and nuanced, and I desperately wanted to understand them, but I knew from experience and conditioning that I might never be successful.

My grandmother, whom we called Nanny, was an amazing woman! Her real name was Lilian and we named our daughter Lily after her and another of Laura's grandmothers. Grandpa Joe was her husband. He was quite honestly a "hot mess" for a lot of his life. They lived on a farm in Lincoln County, Oklahoma and she was always fussing at him to clean up and be presentable. Although she intentionally dressed very plainly, she carried herself with dignity and class. She would quote poetry and other literature while fixing simple, delicious meals. I visited her sister once who was a real estate executive in Denver, Colorado. I often wondered why Nanny never ventured out beyond the borders of Lincoln County. Was she just content to live the simple life? Or, was she just swept off her feet by Little Joe? Sometimes I believe these things, but occasionally I saw something else in her eyes.

I'm making a lot of assumptions, but for some reason I remember her talking about change in her office right before her retirement. They were updating the office and changing things around and she didn't like it. She always liked working, but I think (like many of us) she had an aversion to change. She was afraid of taking risks, and for whatever reason, she didn't get beyond some of those things in her life. I still think she was the greatest grandma ever and I have some of the fondest memories of times at her house; but I wonder what she might have become if she overcame her fears. I wonder what happened to her when she was a little girl. I really would pay anything to talk to little Lily and ask her what she dreamed of becoming and why she was sometimes afraid.

If we could know the nature of our fear and where it originates, maybe we could stop shaming ourselves for being afraid and find a way forward. Sitting in the recliner, I saw myself as a young boy and imagined myself holding that little boy's trembling hand. When I told him that

I had his back, I felt compassion and empathy for him. I heard the voices of the inner critic telling him to "just get over it" and "stop being a baby" but I stepped in between them and had compassion on them both. I told him "you don't have to be afraid because I'm an adult and I'm on your side and we can do this together—I'll go with you." I've seen Laura hold our grandchildren like this. Why can't we have the same compassion for ourselves and our inner child?

I am currently in a training session in the South. Some things about this part of the United States reminds me of where I grew up. One thing that triggered that memory when I saw someone building a "stockade" fence. It's a wood-panel fence that people erect in their backyards. The origin of the fence is from military camps and settlements and goes back to ancient Roman times. These fences make me think about the many ways we build fences in our lives because we are afraid of what is out there.

There are many things physically that we could be afraid of. But, as Masters suggests, "Instead of giving your fears higher walls, give it bigger pastures." I am learning how to make space for things through mindfulness and other contemplative practices. When my tiny backyard of fear is all walled in and protected, it doesn't take much of a noise outside to drive me back indoors to the safety of my sanctuary. Unfortunately, that sanctuary can become a prison where I do not live life as I could. I don't roam the wide-open spaces and explore the vastness of the landscape. I become a prisoner of my own cautiousness. One thing Joey was not afraid of was exploring.

One of the practices that was most helpful for me was focusing. Several of my contemplative companions would lead me to identify where in my body I was holding these feelings of fear. Once identified,

I could sit with the fear much like I would sit with someone grieving or sad or afraid. I did not have to say anything at first--I just had to BE with it. This raised my level or compassion and awareness for what was causing me to be afraid. When there was room for the fear and I wasn't just trying to squash it or remove it or obliterate it, then I could move forward with it responsibly.

When my daughters were growing up, I would tell them to be brave. Many times, it was just a small thing like answering the phone or pulling a tooth. I tried to help them take the next courageous step so that they could see the world from a different vantage point, and then they would be able to imagine a new step. If they could just imagine what felt like fear as energy for proceeding, then next week they would be coaching someone else to "be brave" in this area.

But the other side of the coin for me came from my wife Laura. I wanted them to be bold and courageous, but she reminded me to remember they are afraid and have compassion on them. If I shame them into doing something, then this experience might have the opposite effect from what I had intended. If I have compassion for them, we can take our time and move forward safely and responsibly.

Just like my daughters, I had to tell Joey, "I know you are afraid, and I understand, because I've been afraid too. That's why we are going to do this together. We are just going to take the next step—here we go—I got your back!"

GOING DEEPER WITH MY ANGER

I can probably count on one hand the number of times I had angry outbursts in my adult life. I remember when this would happen, it would scare Laura and she would be very afraid for the children. She warned me that she was not going to tolerate that, but sometimes she would placate me just to calm me down. I was glad that this didn't happen very often because I was taught early in life that this wasn't really the way to do things.

After my experience in the recliner, the inclination to get angry went down. I assumed the reactivity was reduced because I was more aware of what was going on inside me and I could separate those past hurts from the present situation more effectively. But occasionally things still get to me, so I wanted to dig deeper and figure out why I got angry in the first place.

When I was still in elementary school, my father's anger was illustrative to me. I'm not sure if it was ultimately helpful or not. One day, he was transporting a wrestling mat for my team. Someone cut him off and it made him angry. He chased the people down and sort of ran them off the road. I said, "why did you do that?" He didn't say anything and looked like he was about to cry. He turned around and went back and checked on them. Then, I went with him later to take the people some money. I don't remember us having any reasonable dialogue about this and I don't know if it had a positive or negative effect in the long run, I'm just sure it influenced my view of anger. Anger was considered uncool in my family.

Two of my brothers had a temper. What does that mean? It means that they turned games upside down when it did not go their way. I have witnesses. I think all of us had some frustration inside us growing up. I remember rock fights and bar room brawl type of fights. We did not mess around when it came to fighting! I wouldn't really blame it on our parents. My mom pretty much raised us by herself for whatever reasons. But, by the time we got out of high school, the explosive tempers had calmed down. Maybe we were putting all that energy into sports, but then there were an interesting couple of Thanksgiving dinners years later that I still cannot explain.

My mom's children have all moved around quite a bit in their adult lives. Most of them like to do their own thing for Christmas, so Thanksgiving has been the one of the few times when all of us brothers and sisters get together. Thanksgiving is also a potential time when Oklahoma plays Oklahoma State in the Bedlam series. Half of my family is Oklahoma fans and the other is Oklahoma State. We literally sometimes kind of split up to watch the game for good reason. One year, we tried watching it together, but when it went the wrong way, the guy that turned over the board games, got a little too upset, probably because I was trash talking him. I was just as mad as him, but I expressed it a little differently.

The trouble with the way my family does it is that we really do not talk about what makes us angry. It is not acceptable to get too "worked up." That just doesn't work with that many people and I don't think we know how to have a good argument. But, is it good for it not to be okay to get angry? Are there not times when I should be angry? It might be possible that we just miss out on little things that might have been.

When I think about the things that make me angry, it is just a few things; so, I wanted to see if I could make sense of them. But before that, I think it's important to realize that all anger is not bad. If we are excessively outwardly angry, I imagine it pushes things like empathy and vulnerability down into our shadow. Similarly, a distorted belief that we should never be angry or tight-fistedly control our anger probably pushed that very anger down into our shadow to come out sideways later. My siblings and I are probably a mixture of these two things at times, but I want to focus on myself and where I find myself in the past few years.

I have always had an aversion to bullies. The only real fights that I have been in were with bullies. I did not like when the heavy-set boy that was a year older than me was picking on people in Junior high, so I knocked him down and scared him just enough for him to quit. Next when another kid in Junior High told on me, I was angry because he did not work it out with me directly, so I beat him up after school. I may have been on both sides of the bully aisle that day. In high school, someone was picking on the board game flipper and I punched him a few times. In college, there was a guy trying to force his way into our dorm room and I took him down. I was not all that tough, but it drove me crazy when people that had an advantage used that advantage to push people around—I wanted to teach them a lesson.

I felt this same rage later in life with things like Facebook. When I would talk about my plant-based lifestyle, I hoped it would encourage people to learn about it and change. I'll admit some of my posts were provocative, but most people just ignored, agreed or unfriended me. I was a little obnoxious like any new disciple. But, occasionally, people would get aggressive. I think they were just threatened by me essentially saying they were wrong. That wasn't what I was trying to do, but none-the less, I have often found myself in these "debates."

Occasionally, when people are mean and start calling names, it would make me extremely angry and I would lose some of my ability to be civil. Since doing the shadow work, I respond to very few cases and only the most severe. For some reason, when challenged even simply in conversation, I saw this almost as seriously as someone attacking me physically. I'm like my youngest daughter, I do a lot of research before discussing things online. So, when people challenged me aggressively, I used to think "Do they think I'm stupid?" Often, I would see it as another wave of rejection. They were just rejecting my idea, but I could not separate the two.

As I mentioned before, I have literally never been picked for a team. I always started at lower levels of companies and worked my way up. I was chosen in churches a few times, but mainly because I worked extremely hard at fitting in. I would do any kind of lower-level work just to prove to them that I belonged there. Recently, a counselor suggested to me that I use those types of mind games to my advantage. Because I don't believe that they will accept me, they don't and then I use it as motivation to surprise them. It has become a self-fulfilling kind of circle of craziness that I've lived in most of my life. The shadow work helped because I learned to be more authentic and accept myself first.

But because it wasn't okay to be outwardly angry, I handled most of these things that I was angry about inside. Laura could tell when I was keeping something bottled up, but most people could not. I remember one of my co-workers calling me a "duck-on-water." I said to him and my GM one day, "I don't know what you are thinking." He said essentially, "What about you?" (like it was impossible to tell what I was thinking). I felt pretty good the other day when someone said, "You look angry." That is good, because I was, and it was not even that big of a deal. It's okay for me to show people how I feel. If they can't deal with it, then maybe it's their problem or we both can work on communicating better. But I must believe that it is almost never better to stuff it down.

I may always have inclinations. I think it's good to have proclivity towards injustice. I hope I always get a little upset about that. But when I keep it inside, it will probably come out in the wrong way at the wrong time. I also can't just blow up at every little thing that makes me angry. What I can do is to be aware of my shadow and what is there. What are the hurts of my past and how am I inclined to act? Knowing this helps me respond instead of reacting and possibly to respond more with compassion rather than judgment.

In that fateful weekend I couldn't see little Joey that felt like he was being tortured. He was angry but he really didn't know why. I was angry because I couldn't control the situation and because I didn't understand what was going on. I was angry and it wasn't okay to be angry. So, my shame and anger and confusion got all mixed together. It is hard to describe, but I felt like my inner child was being bullied, but it was because I had not stood up for him before. He had some things to say and he never got to say them. Now internally, I was a wreck.

If the inner critic was preaching anything that day, it was saying, *"You are not enough. You've worked on all this stuff before. You're over 50 years old and you haven't got this figured out. Everyone else has this stuff figured out, you shouldn't be wrestling with this. And people are just going to keep rejecting you because you are different and weird. Who do you think you are?"*

I'm thankful I was able to step into that space that day. I not only saw that Joey was scared and confused and wounded, but I also saw the futility of the critic. Neither one of them had a good prescription for my anger. I had to realize something I intellectually already knew about anger.

From time to time, it would have to be okay for me to be angry. My authentic voice would have to be heard occasionally. I could be angry without harboring anger and I was beginning to see how people were not necessarily rejecting me just because they didn't follow through or they weren't ready for my ideas.

As I shuffle back through the years of my life, it's baffling to recall all the shaming messages that adults used to control us. Religious messages like "Good Christians don't act like that" affect us probably deeper than we know. Sometimes when we're mad, we have a good reason to be.

In the future, whether I'm making a point on Facebook or talking to my grandchildren, what I hope to be is more authentic and vulnerable. If someone hurts me, I hope to be able to tell them about it without having to retaliate. When my grandchildren upset me, I hope I can express this to them compassionately without having to run them off the road in any way.

GOING DEEPER WITH MY BYPASSING

The period in my life when I sat in the recliner was an interesting time in my life. I had previously walked away from a denomination that I had been associated with most of my life. I am very grateful for many of the lessons it taught me. I can honestly say that I was loved and cared for many of the years I spent there. I have a deep appreciation for many aspects of the faith. And, even though I was wounded and experienced things that I now want to work through, there are many things to celebrate about where I came from. It is sort of like how I feel about my family.

I had also adopted a lot of new practices. Most of these were somewhat contemplative and involved my focus on solitude and breathing more than words and actions. I was finding peace by myself as well as more of a comfort around people. I had found some new friends at a larger church where I could sort of hide out, but also with the Sisters at Atchison, KS where I was involved in spiritual formation. All of it was a little more mystical, a lot less certain and somehow a bit deeper and wider for me. Don't ask me to explain that better, because it's about as good as I can do.

Adopting new spiritual practices can move us in directions that are positive. Sometimes they help us understand things better. Often our new practices can bring an excitement that has been missing. But, most often if they are legitimate, they open us up and expose areas that we have been avoiding. The phrases and practices that originally caused us to avoid these areas is what many term, *spiritual bypassing*.

Ever since man invented religion to help him understand God, he has spent a lot of time trying to transcend this earth and avoid the physical realities of life. To me, spiritual bypassing is using spiritual language or making religious excuses for not doing the hard and difficult work of navigating this world that we live in. We are spiritual beings, but we also must face the hard realities of our woundedness and struggles as humans.

Bypassing is when we exchange something that takes effort and replace it with something easy that sounds good.

My religious background taught me many catch phrases and quoted various Scriptures regularly to avoid having to face things that were difficult or deal with something I didn't understand. So, the best way I can think of to describe this process and what I was going through is to share some of these phrases with you.

My prayer life has certainly evolved in the past few years. My prayer is much more contemplative and slower and quieter. It's way less about asking God for things and much more about becoming and being for me. Prayer to me is a connection to the Divine and to those that I am thinking about when I pray. Recently I noticed that a lot of times when we say, "I'll pray for you," it's really a form of bypassing. Usually what people really need is empathy which sounds more like "that sucks" or "me too" instead of promising to represent them before God.

I think what would be more helpful and healing would be to empathize with the person. Or, maybe we could just sit with them and cry or hold their hand. During my shadow experience, not once did I ask people to "pray for me" or "surround me in prayer" or "go before the throne." I think most of that kind of thing is just spiritual bypassing.

I tend to think God was already there in the room with me and, that day, I could literally feel the presence. There wasn't any need to get a bunch of people to beg him to be there—he was already there—where else would He be? There was no one to impress with spiritual words. It was time to get to work.

I used to tell people "God is in control." It felt very spiritual to say that. My boss even got through a tough time because I told him that. But the reason he got through the tough time was because he also told all his employees to buckle down. And they all believed they could get through it or that they didn't have any other options, so they emerged on the right side of the equation. God probably cares much more about character and how they treated each other than whether they won that financial victory. Luckily, they didn't really believe God is in control or they wouldn't have done the work necessary to save the company.

I don't think God controls us because control is a result of fear and I don't think the Divine would be afraid. In my book, Apparent Faith, I discussed this topic. I don't think control does anything noble because there are many things more important than things turning out like we want. But the biggest reason I no longer say, "God is in Control," is because when I say it, I tend to shuck off all my responsibility for whatever I am hoping God will control. Please consider the following statement:

> My unmet needs and my deepest wounds are never going to be addressed until someone stops assuming God will fix them and gets down to the hard work of healing!

Another way to totally abdicate all responsibility is to say, "God has a purpose." I tried to imagine what would have happened if I would have said that on the weekend in question. First, I'm not sure that I would still be married. Next, I'm not sure that I wasn't headed for a nervous breakdown. If God did have a purpose it was to take me down or something sinister like that. Then I would have to add other silly phrases like "this will make you stronger." Religious fix-it people could have piled on at this point. "It will all work out for good in the end," I can hear them say, or the worst ever, "are you sure there's not some sin in your life?" None of those people in my life were trying to hurt me, but none of those phrases ultimately helped me or made the situation any better. They simply bypassed the issue and made all of us feel a little temporary, superficial comfort that didn't last.

The truth about my situation was this. Almost everyone I know has made it a practice to avoid the hard work of getting better, either out of ignorance, stubbornness or pride. These practices by well-meaning people wounded me and my family. I blame the organization and the people of the church, as well as my friends and family and myself. All the while, I understand why they did it, because I know why I did it. That was all we knew how to do. Here I was sitting in a recliner somewhere between suicide, a mental breakdown and a hope that I might get better. At this point, I didn't need a damn religious platitude to bypass my problem. I needed somewhat of a plan, and I needed encouragement to do the hard work necessary.

I think most of the flaws in most religious systems are the beliefs that there are magic solutions to problems, even though I recognize there are miraculous things about life that are hard to explain. Just the fact that our body can seek out and destroy a virus most of the time is amazing. Every cell of our bodies is unbelievably magical. It was important for me to get out of this dependency to bypass the normal physical processes of life for an easy magical answer based loosely on truth and often out of context.

People that study neural pathways and brain function call it *dissociating*. It means to "to disconnect or separate." Spiritual bypassing separates us from our humanity and all its messiness and struggles and pain and It makes us feel good briefly. I noticed many of my faith communities seemed stubbornly determined to be happy;, having said that, sometimes the human condition calls for something different than happiness. Bypassing tries to convince us that we should avoid anything painful and just pray that God would take it away magically. I like when my contemplative friends talk about "sitting" with the things that trouble them. This is at the least a good start. The next step after this is most likely compassion.

Sitting in the recliner, I do not remember uttering a single religious platitude or famous catchphrase to get me through. The spiritual directors that were working with me were too wise for that. I didn't recite any famous prayers. I didn't read any Scripture. I didn't sing any religious songs. I didn't rub any beads or say any mantras. All those things have their place, but what I did in this moment of discovery was something different. I'm not saying it's for everyone, but what I said was, "Okay I'm all in!" And that's where it began.

GOING DEEPER WITH MY VOICE

I was excited when Laura started to *find her voice*. Back in my earlier days, even when I was a little more committed to the man as the primary leader in the home, I still wanted Laura to have equal say and an equal voice. The few times that she gave speeches made me wish she could preach, and I could sit in the audience. She has a more natural speaking voice and she has always had something vital to say. Since I was a preacher and writer, I assumed I was using my voice and nothing much was hindering it. It's amazing how confused we can be in this area. I certainly was.

Please understand I am not talking about introverts and extroverts. I will most likely always be an introvert. I love people, I just don't want them around all the time. I have friends that are extroverts and introverts, people that talk a lot and people that talk a little. I know natural-born speakers and people that struggle to speak well, especially in public. Even with writers, there is a great mixture of personalities and temperaments. I think finding our voice is something a little deeper than just what we have proclivity toward. In its simplest form, finding our voice may be that we are learning not only who we are but also learning how to express who we are through our words and actions.

One thing is for sure. if we don't get to say what we really need to say, our voice goes down into our shadow and we suffer the consequences of that. Like many other things, when our voice gets pushed down into our shadow, usually what we have to say comes out wrong and at inopportune times. When I am not speaking from a place of authenticity, I end up speaking my truth to the wrong people at the wrong times and with the wrong attitude. Why is finding our voice even necessary?

My friend, Mark Karris says,

> "For many of us, it is not just finding our voice, it is sharing it with others that is so powerful. When there is a cacophony of voices all around us, people listening to us helps us feel *safe and alive*. It *validates* our existence and *soothes* our existential angst, especially if we are prone to thinking about our mortality and sheer evaporation from existence in a relatively short period of time. Sharing our voice with others helps us feel *less alone*, more *connected*, and provides tremendous *purpose*. Knowing we are making a difference in the world, knowing that our pain, suffering, and divine gems can help someone else, is hugely *rewarding*."

I thought I started finding my voice in college after I almost failed speech class because I forgot half of my 15-minute final speech. I realized I might have a problem that needed to be addressed. A couple of years later, one of my managers called me into her office and told me I did indeed have a problem. She told me I was smart, but if I didn't figure out how to talk (you know like to people), then my job was going to be in jeopardy. There was a group / class in the same building that helped people get better at things like this and I joined it. It was excruciating at times (think extemporaneous speaking for recluses), but it was helpful. A few years later, I joined a Toastmasters group where I eventually became a leader and won a couple of awards for speaking. Just a short time after that, I accepted a call to pastor a church and the circle of shyness was complete. Well not really, I still shook a little every time I spoke, but I figured that was a good thing.

Did I really find my voice? I always considered myself a somewhat challenging speaker. I liked to "step on people's toes" a little but do it in a nice way. I liked to see them have positive changes in their life from what they heard from my preaching. But, when you are preaching to a congregation and especially the same congregation, you only have so much wiggle room in that process. Although I was challenging people, to a large extent I was mainly telling them what they wanted to hear. I was mainly trying to gain the approval of others and find some satisfaction in it. Sure, I overcame my shyness, but I didn't necessarily find my voice. It might have touched some of Mark's bullet points but not really in any genuine kind of way.

Why didn't I use my voice more effectively in the first half of my life? Did something cause me to believe it didn't matter? My mom's always afraid I'm going to blame stuff on her, but I don't remember my mom directly doing anything dramatic or extremely traumatic, but I do think there are some things that are a little bit significant for a boy that used to hide under the table when people came over.

Like most children during my era, it was common for children to make fun of each other. Bullying was barely even acknowledged. Calling people names and making fun of them was the norm and not the exception. My childhood was full of all different kinds of schools and daycares. When you have thick glasses and you're short and you sometimes wear funny clothes, it's just kind of natural that you get picked on. At least it was in the time I grew up. Speaking up or speaking in front of the class was just another way to get made fun of.

I don't know about anyone else, but I was a little mischievous when I was a boy. Some of the things I remember especially were in Junior High. While attending a private school, I learned how to steal candy at the store, throw water balloons at cars and eventually smoked a few cigarettes. I didn't like smoking that much, but I adopted smokeless tobacco and retained that habit for the next 30 years or so.

The question is not how bad the things we do are, but how did the adults respond to us. When I was in Junior High, the strategy seemed to be either spanking (hitting) or shaming. I remember distinctly the day my mother realized that spanking no longer worked. It was the day I told her, "that didn't hurt."

The question about spanking is not whether it works. Spanking gets results. But, does it get the "right" results? What are we teaching kids about the world when we spank them? Just because spanking gets results doesn't mean it accomplishes anything noble. I know this because eventually it stops working. It either creates underlings that eventually aren't afraid of you anymore (like me) or it finally breaks that person and they will never be the human being they could have been without intense therapy. The people that say, "Our parents spanked us, and we turned out okay," do not really want people to respond to that statement. Did they?

The adults of my era are not much different. They have moved away from spanking because you can literally get in more trouble for doing it. Some have realized, it is not that effective in the long run, just for the moment. Most adults eventually find themselves using shame to control their children. In practice it's not all that different. It works to control people quite well for the immediate situation; but it creates all kinds of problems down the road. Shaming children may gain control of the classroom, but the students are possibly wounded afterwards. In my estimation that's not a good solution for the long-term.

In Junior High, my teachers could spank me and shame me. They did both with a lot of enthusiasm it seemed. It controlled me for a little while, but in the long run, it just made me that much more rebellious. Day by day, I felt dirtier and more "sinful." My view of God was also slipping into a God that was just disappointed in me and just wanted me to write sentences on the chalkboard, so he did not have to punish me more sternly. In His eyes, what I really deserved was much worse, and I knew this because it got reinforced "religiously."

Nothing in my life really motivated me to find my voice. A couple of times when I found my voice, I got my mouth washed out with soap. The adults in my life generally didn't care what I had to say. Everything I did seemed to disappoint God, so I was sure He didn't care what I had to say. And there were consequences when we talked too much in class, or spoke our mind, or even when we had the wrong look on our face. The first teacher I remembered listening to me was our English teacher, Mrs. Allen, who taught me how to write creatively, but that was in high school and by then my voice was far down in my shadow.

Most of the other systems I grew up in were also religious. Religion is often very shame based. It's different from people that make fun of you. Religion doesn't overtly call you names … or does it? Religion usually sets up the premise that we are worthless without whatever solution it is offering. When even my righteous acts are considered *filthy rags* and I'm labeled as *sinner* and a *wretch* who falls short of the mark, it's hard to gain a lot of confidence even if someone did redeem me. Because, as Laura implied, there is still a God out there that is an asshole and it is my fault that he is that way. I mean, they let me say a testimony about how God saved me from all that, but it's hard to feel it deep down when you keep getting pounded every week with the negative side of it. In that system, what do I really have to say in a testimony? "I'm lucky?"

Christianity is my background, so it is what I can speak to. Most religions have an unspoken rule that it's better if we stay kind of homogenous in our religious tribes, and Christianity is no exception. Isn't that what belief statements are all about? If we are going to be a group, we need to agree to believe mostly in the same things. We must stay somewhat alike or they will not know how to recognize us, not to mention that there might be some type of divine retribution when we do not operate under the umbrella of that group's manifesto. One of the problems is that there are between 9,000 and 33,000 protestant denominations worldwide, each with their own system of keeping people the same—see the problem? My point is that it doesn't promote people having a unique voice and usually you get punished for it.

The first type of retribution is *rejection*. A few years ago, when I changed some of my beliefs, most of my friends stopped talking to me. A few of them were brave enough to discuss it somewhat online. I have discovered the number of things we can disagree on are exactly two. They usually argue for a while about the one issue, then they say something like "Let me get this straight Karl. You don't believe in this issue (the way I do) *and* you don't believe in this other issue (the way I do)?" I know when they say that, we are just about done. I am getting ready to get shunned. Most times, I don't even get to talk to them, so I admire the ones that do take the time to make the call that I'm a heretic.

Even though most religious people won't admit it, they are apt to also respond to differing beliefs and people that find their voice with *hostility.* I wish I could confirm that this isn't true, but my tribe (the Christians) were often the most combative to those that were upsetting their stability or challenging their beliefs. Why? Because "wrong" beliefs are considered cancer and cancer must be treated aggressively. We don't want it affecting the whole *body.* If I wanted to find my voice, it would be okay for me to speak my truth as long as it stays within the group's doctrinal boundaries (this particular one of the other 9,000—let's just use the low number).

As I said before, it is tough to find your voice as a pastor, even though you get to write and speak all the time. I was thinking, along with a friend of mine, about book sales in my current situation. I said, "If I were in my old denomination, I could sell a lot of books just because I was in that denomination." He reminded me though that they would not read what I am writing now, and I would not want to write what they would find as acceptable. I think finding our voice separates us in a way and probably most of us love our certainty and don't want to get off whatever track we are on. The trouble is that we sacrifice our voice.

I think all of us want to find this unique voice that is us. But how do I find it? I think it begins with telling ourselves the right things. We won't be motivated to find our voice and express it when we think of ourselves as worthless. I don't agree any more with religious systems that promote the devaluing of any human beings. I also must get in front of my inner critic and, with compassion, tell him to knock it off.

Finding my voice means understanding deeply who I am. It is not just about what I have to say, it's about my self hidden deep within me. It's about what little Joey and the much older Karl has to say, but it's also about who they are and what they stand for. It's not about the belief system they were assigned because of their circumstances, and it's not about the practice they stayed in because of shame and other pressures of that system. It is about who they really are and what they can share with the world. At least for the ones that earn the right to hear it.

It is important for me to remember not to argue with people that disagree. Just because someone engages me doesn't mean they are ready to hear my truth. If someone provokes me, it may be much better to turn the other cheek and wait until they are ready to hear it. It may be something about where to cast your pearls, but it is mainly about my self-respect for the importance of my voice. It matters and I matter—I want to be truly heard and understood.

I believe I will get unique chances to share my voice. But it's got to be my voice. When I know who I am, I will most likely know what my voice needs to say. But, with a little mindfulness or prayer or just a little time, I may also be able to discover who my voice was honed for.

GOING DEEPER WITH MY CRITIC

"Kids can be cruel," is one of the things we say to each other. Children are certainly direct. They tend to say what they are thinking and sometimes that is hurtful. Recently we've begun to have better discussions about bullying because we have realized that those hurtful things that children say to each other aren't just inevitable realities of life but rather something that has been allowed to plant trauma in young minds even though it might not necessarily have been meant to cause harm.

Sometimes children and adults don't know what to do with this childish behavior so we store it away so we can get on with our lives. Of course, the trouble is that this subterranean trauma comes back to visit us later.

Often people like teachers and parents that are supposed to mold and shape us go too far and use shame as a motivator instead of encouragement or something more useful. I know exactly how it happens. As a parent, I got frustrated. I would go from teaching, to nagging, and when that didn't work, I resorted to a tactic that always got immediate results—shaming. Shame is like harsh discipline, in that it gets quick responses and immediate movement toward the goal, but it doesn't achieve a good long-term result. Again, it's because something is stored away inside of us and eventually it comes out in a much more problematic way.

I suppose there have been hundreds of critics in my life. When people that I didn't care about criticized me, it stung briefly but didn't stay with me too long. I didn't care that much about what they thought. But, when people that I cared about shamed me, it often stung deeply.

I would not say it was the harshest voices in my life that wounded me, because sometimes it was the more subtle messages that stayed with me longer. Sometimes it was what they said—sometimes it was what they didn't say. And occasionally, it was just a look that made me think *I'm not even worth a response from them.* I can't remember most of the critics in my life directly; but, probably one of the most prohibitive forces in my life is the critic that lives inside me.

We all have that inner critic that speaks up from time to time. Much like an impatient parent would talk to a young growing boy or girl, the inner critic within us speaks to the child within us. My friend, Mark Karris defines this critic as,

> "an amalgam of external voices of others (including culture) that get internalized and takes on a life of its own. The harsher the voices that get internalized, the harsher the critic."

This is not the Devil or Satan and it probably won't help us to spiritualize or bypass it. As I discussed previously, avoiding what is inside us just proliferates and prolongs the problem. Before I talk about how I dealt with this issue in the recliner, I thought I would share some of the ways the critic shows up in my life. If you take some time to go inward, I bet you can see some similarities in your life.

As you might have noticed earlier in this book, rejection is a magnified issue in my life. I say, "magnified" because it has a lot to do with how I perceive it. Girls most likely were not rejecting me, they were probably usually saying to me subtly "*You're just not the one for me*", but I probably interpreted it with lots of shaming messages that I stored away for later reference. I once broke up with a girl because her dad was mean, but she probably took it way more personal than that.

Even though Laura and I have been married for 31 years, not all our years have been blissful and easy. We never learned how to openly communicate effectively, so we often unnecessarily, and even unintentionally shamed each other. This very often formed around intimacy. Because our toxic religion with its fear tactics and negative messages got all wrapped up in our sex life, then we didn't communicate effectively about it. So, instead of working through it, we just delayed it until I found myself sitting in a recliner wondering what the hell happened! That weekend was not about sex, but it was about rejection and true intimacy.

The critic screamed at me on the weekend in question. It told me that I wasn't important to Laura just because her sister was over. I was convinced she was abusing me. We didn't have a horrible, dysfunctional relationship before this weekend, but we had experienced these types of eruptions occasionally throughout the years. I thought maybe we could get through this one, but what if the next one was worse? I imagined that this is how many marriages end.

My dad was absent, at least emotionally, from what I remember. It seemed like he was trying at times, but it didn't seem like he had the skills and often he didn't have the inclination to totally be there emotionally. I remember that part of my healing experience was to say to my dad (who has been gone for years), "I don't need your approval!" This helped me greatly, but I am quite sure my father never said directly, "I don't approve of you." It's just not the kind of thing he would have said. But somehow subtle messages in his infidelity and lack of dedication, told me that I was not that most important thing in his life and my adolescent mind stored it away as *I'm not enough to be primary*—I think it affected me greatly but I don't think I've completely sorted it out yet.

One of the ways this issue surfaces for me is that the messages the critic says to me is "you can do better." It doesn't seem that awkward on the surface, but it gets translated into an unrealistic drive that tells me I am always behind. As I write this book (which will probably be my fourth), the second book is just finishing editing. Laura has told me, "Before you finish one project, you are on to the next big thing." It's true! I always feel like I'm so far behind because I'm searching for approval or recognition that I never quite found.

My brother and I had literally hundreds of trophies and medals growing up—I would do almost anything for a medal or certificate and it continues into my adulthood through diplomas and other things that promise to quench the thirst for approval. After the day in the recliner, I have begun to interrupt the diatribe of the critic with messages like, "I am enough, and I don't need his approval or my dad's!"

Friends and family often brought judgement to me cloaked as something different. In fact, I think the intention may have been quite honorable. I think my friends and family wanted me to make good choices. I think we even told our children to make good choices. Of course, it got translated into something harsher. What I heard from these people was not just a wish for me to make a good decision—I heard that I better not make even one mistake because one of the primary rules of any organization or family is don't embarrass us.

When I stole a cassette tape in high school and got caught, I realized I had committed the cardinal rule—I embarrassed the group and shamed them and myself (I'm pretty sure the principal said something like that before he made me feel real pain). The school got over it quickly, but I didn't, and the corporal punishment didn't do anything to reform me, it just drove the shame deeper inside me.

After this situation, the critic screamed out,"*You really must impress them now—you are even further behind as the new kid at this school*". I realized later, that is why I stole the tape in the first place. Now that I had a bad reputation, I had to work extra hard to make them show me their approval, unfortunately I did that in all the wrong ways. I kind of wish my principal would have shown me grace and love instead of beating me. It just kind of made me angry and didn't really resolve anything in my life. This chapter in my life didn't begin to close until I stepped in front of the critic and began to address him more directly.

Just a side note. Looking back on all my years of parenting. My children made the best choices only by imitating what they saw me do. When I tried to shame them, it didn't really work and probably left them with their own problems to resolve.

Religion also played the same kind of role in my life. The church organizations, even when they were love based, worried a lot about being embarrassed and whether I was conforming to the norms of their society. Religious people would come to me "worried" or "concerned" about me (and maybe sometimes they genuinely were). Most often they were simply afraid that something I might do could cause an upset in their normal operations.

What this said to me through my inner critic was things like "*we don't trust you*" and "*we don't think you are smart enough to make good decisions.*" Hmmm ... I just realized I had some similar conversations with my children when they were teenagers. Since somehow my children were a little wiser than me, a lot of times they confronted me about this, but a lot of it was similar to walking around in a tornado and trying to find shelter and direction all at the same time. Like adolescence, parenting is also as frightening as it is disorienting and I'm often surprised that we survived it with somewhat of a reasonable outcome. Just like I still remember some of the more terrifying storms in Oklahoma growing up, I still remember some of these messages I internalized from well-meaning religious people.

There were only a couple of people at each of the churches we pastored that seriously left me with ammunition for my critic. However, the religious *systems* I have observed and been involved with have been much more damaging. Most of the time, it was oddly enough attached to misapplication of words found in the Bible. It starts with the basic assumption that we are essentially bad! I talked about this in my previous book, *Apparent Faith*. I no longer believe that I was originally bad like the preacher told me when I was 7.

But the critic still remembers some of those messages and recants them to me when I am feeling down. He says, "*You are not really that good anyway.*" Again, I no longer attribute that to Satan or The Devil—it's just the residual from the first half of my life coming back to haunt me, literally.

Religion often adds to this message a steady drumbeat of how I "miss the mark." While it may be true that God has a higher ideal of how I can love him and my neighbor, I don't think it affects his approval (remember that one) and his love for me. I don't even think he needs to redeem me or for me to repent before he starts loving me. He is always there (not absent) and his desire is for me.

The critic says, "yes but you need to start with the fact that you are rejected," and I must intercede with the love of the Divine to tell him he's wrong. I have always been loved, I will always be loved, and I am accepted unconditionally. I was accepted before, during and after I stole the cassette tape.

Religion wants to create a timeline where I was horrible, then I was redeemed. The trouble comes when I don't perform the way I think I should, or the way I think the church thinks I should or the way the people at the church perceive I should. When this happens. the critic steps up to the microphone and tells how unworthy I am of anyone's love, much less God's love. In these moments I don't feel like being in the presence of the Divine or hanging around super spiritual people. I just want to crawl in a hole and hope people don't notice me as much.

Some of my critic's favorite mantras are as follows:

- You will be rejected by them (they always do)
- You are behind (you need to work extra hard to catch up)
- You are different (I mean just look at your glasses)
- You are too silly (we don't have time for that)
- You need to impress them (don't be selfish, they are what matters)
- You can't let them really see you (they won't be impressed or like you)

Every one of these messages is a combination of messages from my past, mixed with my misapplication and misinterpretation that only leads me normally to further bury them in my subconscious. Some of them obviously were from mean people, more often they were from people with good intentions, including myself. I've kept them for a long time—in a way, these thoughts are my best friends. They're familiar. They are comfortable in a way. Just like the adults in my life I don't want them to go away—I just want them to behave!

The primary way I began to deal with the critic was to realize that these messages very well were like friends to me. They were not the kind of friends that inspired me to greatness, but they were a part of me, and I could not just exterminate them or cut them out like you would with surgery. I tried that once and it just left a lot of scar tissue and didn't solve the issue. What I have been learning is that I must listen to the critic and try to understand what it was initially trying to warn me about. What pain surrounded this issue? When did I initially become concerned with things like approval? Where did the message go awry?

When I face my critic with love and compassion, I can then invite him / her to just take a rest. Then I gently take my child by the hand and let him know that he's already approved and he's not going to embarrass anyone by being silly and people may laugh at him (but that's okay and they probably were just uncomfortable when they said those things). *"I know it hurts you, but you don't need their approval anyway",* I say to him again. *"The first people we represent are ourselves. The Divine is with us not waiting for us to perform—the people that made you feel worthless were also confused and scared like the critic over there. We got this—I got your back."*

GOING DEEPER WITH MY PAIN

Two-A-Day practices were common for high school football in the South. It is a big deal and almost everyone in my high school was on the team to ensure that we had enough to play on Friday nights. My friend and I worked at a local business where we did a lot of physical work, and we still were required to go to practice twice a day every weekday in the summer. At the end of the day, I just wanted to lay down and just sleep for a couple of days.

There were only a couple of ways to make the pain go away. I could quit and never really know any of the thrills of being a part of the team. But, after a couple of days, the pain would subside—of course, then I would have different issues to face. I would be ashamed that I let the team down and that I would not get to do what I had done every year since the 3rd grade. Giving into pain causes us to miss opportunities. There is very little that doesn't have some minor pain at the least.

I could have also numbed the pain in some way. The trouble with numbing the pain, is it numbs everything else. Not only would the pain be gone, but also the joy and excitement that comes with being fully alive and fully functional would also be minimized or eliminated. I'm glad I didn't choose this option. Even though it might give me temporary relief, I'm glad I got to feel everything including the pain.

Really, the only way to deal with pain is to lean into it. It still hurts and sometimes it hurts more for a little while, but eventually the pain subsides, and we become stronger. The coaches knew it would build our stamina and our strength so that we could be ready for the battle that was ahead of us. Whether it's running a race, or playing a game, or just trying to get through life, eventually we will have to make ourselves lean into the pain in order to make progress. What I have observed from my life is when we avoid all pain, eventually everything is painful. If I do not walk occasionally, eventually it hurts just to walk upstairs.

Even though the time I spent in the recliner didn't involve anything physical, it most definitely involved pain. All the areas that I had neglected were now being exercised simultaneously. When I said that I was all in, the hard, painful work started and continued throughout the day. Everything I read and thought about and "heard" that day caused me a little pain. It was like the two-a-day practice where I found muscles, that I didn't even know I had. My heart felt like it was going to beat out of my chest, as I encountered one painful obstacle after another. It felt like running a marathon without training for it.

Since then, I have tried to lean into the pain daily. What it feels like is running after you have spent some time getting in shape. It still hurts a little. But what I have leaked is to step into the pain enough that I can face the struggles without collapsing and wanting to quit. At other times in my life, I was not able to step up to the painful things in my life, and I kept them hidden. In a way, all the things in this manuscript are those painful things that I didn't face because they were too painful at the time.

Just like going to the gym or eating right or getting some necessary counseling, we must expose the painful things and acknowledge them so that they become a conscious concern instead of a hidden unknown that surprises us at the wrong time. It is similar to how I started throwing my back out later in life because I was unwilling to lean into the discomfort of keeping my core in shape. The pain comes in one way or another. It's better to be proactive.

Most of the pain I have always been fearful of leaning into is the shame of feeling less than other people. If I'm brave, I know that being in relationship means I risk feeling the pain of rejection. The pain of loneliness remains sometimes even when I am brave. Often, I will work hard enough to be accepted on a surface level, but I don't take the risks necessary to be what I genuinely feel would fulfill me. I do what it takes to make people like me, but I do not do the hard work of being authentic.

There are many things that I am learning to lean into. Just like the two-a-day practices, they aren't always fun to experience, but I can see a larger goal ahead and I can imagine the time when they are not as hard because I've conditioned myself to be able to endure the tougher road. If we are willing to do the work necessary, I think there comes a time when we can play the game of life with somewhat a sense of ease. We will likely still be tired and frustrated at the end of day, but we will also feel the exhilaration of playing the game knowing that we leaned into the discomfort and did the best we could.

But, now that I have leaned into the pain of my past, I have discovered somewhat of a new way to live. It is the understanding and practice of *being*. In the chapters that follow, I hope to somehow put this way of knowing and way of being into a readable format where you the reader can experience what I am experiencing in this season of my life. It feels beautiful to me and I hope you can get a sense of a way of life that is closer to being *authentic* and being *present*. I describe it as being *where you are* (presence) and *being who you are* (authenticity).

I do not claim to have everything figured out. The way I am attempting to *be* is not a rote mimicking of anything I see in the world. I am finished with living my life that way. It is an attempt to be true to myself and live in the place where I find myself. Again, it is presence and authenticity. Maybe you would like to judge for yourself, or maybe you would like to simply come along on the journey with me. I do not promise you anything, but I invite you to be yourself and find your own way.

As we journey together, we most likely will realize we are not always on the same path, but as our paths cross, we can encourage each other and learn from each other and we might just discover that we are a part of something bigger that touches us all in similar ways.

PART III

Learning to Be

BEING WITH CRISIS

As I write the words to this chapter, the world is amid what most would describe as a crisis. It is described on a government website in my home state as, "an outbreak of respiratory disease caused by a novel (new) coronavirus that was first detected in many locations internationally, including in the United States." The virus has been named "SARS-CoV-2" and the disease it causes has been named "coronavirus disease 2019" (abbreviated "COVID-19").[3] COVID-19 is spread through contact and has quickly spread throughout the world even to my hometown of Rock Port, MO. My Facebook feed today includes my mother's disappointment that the virus has reached her hometown. The numbers change daily, so I won't bore you with the numbers, but it's safe to say we are in the middle of a pandemic.

Of course, there are some that are blatantly dismissing it as a crisis. They want to make it something spiritual or call it a conspiracy. For the sake of brevity and because I'm part baby boomer, for now I will just dismiss them and move on with what I'm trying to accomplish here. For me, I was just isolated from my job for 27 days, my daughter has been quarantined in her home for 2 weeks and we hear of new updates every day. Most of the people that dismissed this pandemic have been slowing arising from their slumber, including me.

I don't know about you, but people like me have a coping strategy we like to employ. When something unique happens, we try to normalize or minimize it. If I can somehow tie what is happening to

---

[3] https://health.mo.gov/living/healthcondiseases/communicable/novel-coronavirus/

something that happened in the past or if I can make it seem smaller in my mind than it actually is, then it won't be as scary or I won't have to make any changes in my life to adjust to the changes that are impending. Even though I like adventure, I like planned adventures and what I am discovering is that this is a living contradiction or maybe even an oxymoron. And, to make it worse, Dr. Mary Jeppsen states the following:

"There have never been times like these ... unprecedented"[4]

The situation we find ourselves is indeed like nothing most of us have ever seen or experienced in our lifetime. I have very few reference points for dealing with this crisis, so as I start to experience my part in this pandemic let me just state a few guidelines that I am building from. Primarily, *it is okay not to be okay* and *it is okay to feel what you feel*. Any time we shame ourselves or others for feeling what we feel, we just create many more problems and we have enough challenges. We don't need to add guilt or shame or more despair to the equation. It's enough on its own merit. The other thing I would share with you is what my friend Dr. Paul Fitzgerald says, "Don't waste a good crisis." So, hopefully that is what I am doing here.

Be Where You Are

Mrs. Beaty is one of the teachers I remember from private school. I remember her as kind and compassionate. She was probably patient also if she had to deal with me in those days, but every time someone

---

[4] Gleaned from an online conversation on March 28, 2020.

talks about school, the classroom I picture is hers. Back then, teachers took roll calls. They would call out your name and you could either say "here" or "present." Both meant the same thing—you were in the seat that was assigned to you. The word *present* did not mean what we now commonly refer to as at least some form of awareness and sort of a single focus on something.

Jesus seemed to have this presence. Contrary to popular belief, I don't think he necessarily was always impressive, but I do believe he was always present. As a boy, when he was in the temple, he was fully present with the teachers and didn't realize that the caravan for home had already left. He was fully engaged with what was most important and not distracted by other people's agenda for him. When he was in the boat, he was fully engaged in the task at hand even when the task was taking a nap. When he was in the garden, he was in the garden and not a million miles away. When he went away to pray, he was fully present in prayer and not reliving the past or dreading the future.

Over the past 18 months, I have been doing some very simple, physical work. People often ask me, "So, what's the plan?" By this, I think they are struggling to see me as doing this physical work for anything more than a temporary stent. I've been an office worker for much of my adult life. The story of the last few years takes a long time to delineate and where I think this might be going is hard to describe, so I just say this:

This is what I am doing today.

I say this because that is exactly what I say inside my head. If I look beyond the boundaries of the current day, or sometimes hour, I may become frightened of the future or regretful about the past. The best place to be is in the present. It's really the only time we can truly live in. Our minds typically are in a hundred places at once. Often, we are absent from the moment we are participating in. There is a time to plan, but even those plans are subject to change. There is also a time to go back and do some necessary repair work. It can be fruitful; we just cannot live there. The only place we can live is in the here and now.

So, I say to myself, "This is what I am doing now" and "this is where I am." One of my new favorite theologians, Thich Nhat Hanh says, "The present moment is filled with joy and happiness if you are attentive, you will see it."[5] This is how I want to live the rest of my life—in the present moment, experiencing joy and happiness because I was paying attention.

When Mrs. Beaty would say, "Mr. Forehand" and I would say, "president" or answer in a funny voice, she would exclaim "Mr. Forehand just say 'here' or 'present'." When Mrs. Beaty said *present*, she wanted to know if I was there. When Laura says, "Are you here?" she means "Are you present?" Let's all come back to the present and live in the only time we can!

Be Who You Are

In the Bible, there is an incident described that I would describe as something similar to a drone strike.[6] To make a long story short, Elijah the prophet and King Ahaziah get into a struggle about whether the

---

5 https://www.goodreads.com/quotes/259142-the-present-moment-is-filled-with-joy-and-happiness-if

6 2 Kings 1

king is respecting God. Elijah responds to the king's lack of respect for God with calling down fire from heaven (like a drone strike) and wipes out the soldiers in successive waves (50 at a time) until Elijah (and apparently God) finally shows some mercy. It seems like a bit of an overreaction, to say the least, but it leaves me with a lot of questions.

The question I ask is, "Is this what God is really like—does he really end people's life just for disrespecting him?" To me that sounds like a gangster or a mob boss more than a loving, restorative God. It seems retributive and even childish, not wise like I imagine The Divine to be. The other big question I ask is, "Is this how we are supposed to be?" Are we supposed to be retributive to those who oppose God or don't consult him first or believe in him? Apparently, the Israelites believed in the drone strike god because there is another reference to it in Luke chapter nine.

After the transfiguration, Jesus is traveling to Jerusalem and sends messengers ahead to secure lodging for their visit. When the Samaritan village was unwelcoming, James and John questioned, "Lord, do you want us to call fire down from heaven to destroy them?"[7] Apparently, the common belief about their identity was that when someone stands in our way, we remove them from our path in the quickest and most efficient way. That was their understanding of *who they were*. Even though Jesus' teaching was completely contrary to this, they still clung to the ancient misunderstanding about God and what the people of God are like.

---

7   Luke 9:54

Jesus rebukes them. In some manuscripts, "You don't know what kind of spirit you belong to." If I could interpret a little, I would suggest that the battle is between the spirit of retribution and spirit of restoration. Jesus demonstrated his love and mercy toward the Samaritans (the sworn enemy of the Jews) several times. When Peter tried the way of retribution with his sword in the garden, Jesus rebuked him and basically told him, "that's not who we are."

Most of us like Peter are just trying to fit in. We want to be significant and we look to other people for models of how to get where we think we are going. James and John wanted to be like Elijah that represented the prophets. I can relate to that because I love the poets and the prophets and often lump them together. But in our desire to be significant, we must remember that the one basic requirement is we first must be who we are. We must be authentic. One of my oldest daughter's favorite quotes used to be Oscar Wilde's statement:

> "Most people are other people. Their thoughts are someone else's opinions, their life is a mimicry, their passions a quotation." [8]

I have a tattoo on my arm of a couple of Chinese characters. The characters are a Mandarin word about authenticity. It literally means, "Real." That is my prayer for the second half of my life and my hope for the world. I want us to be who we are.

Maybe this pause in our lives will cause us to consider living differently. Maybe we can get out of the patterns we have become accustomed to and decide what is important and what is not. Hopefully

---

[8] https://www.goodreads.com/quotes/317-most-people-are-other-people-their-thoughts-are-someone-else-s

our lives will become much simpler by determining what is truly necessary and what is window dressing.

My hope is that we will learn to be where we are and be who we are!

Being in Crisis

by Karl Forehand

Just being present in the place that I am,
    seems absurd when the world is in tatters.
But the more that we see, the more that we know,
    it's really the main thing that matters.

Just being real to the people I see,
    seems minor when the world is a burning.
But knowing myself and being myself,
    is the best thing to take on my journey.

BEING WITH PROPHETS AND POETS

Laura many times has a better sense about social media than I do. She tells me often that I need to "break up" with people on Facebook. In the end I agree with her, but I still have some roots from past religious experiences that believe I can change people. These people also believe the same thing about me. I've learned to weed out those people early on because they often have agendas that either don't interest me or would only take me back to spiritual infancy that I am trying to distance myself from. At the least, it will end in an argument.

These people generally want to "speak" into my life, and they are hoping for an audience that fuels their narcissistic endeavors. Maybe, it's not always true, but my experience teaches me it is just better to avoid them altogether. Engaging with them either ends with an argument or with them condemning me for some vague thing that isn't even true. With that said, I have nothing but admiration and respect for those that are truly prophetic and have something to say to the world. I lump them together, the poets and the prophets.

These people, the *poets and the prophets,* are quite the opposite from the people I mentioned before. They do not seek to be honored or recognized as much as they like to give what they have been given. They have a song to sing or word to say, but because they don't always understand what it is they are trying to share, it is always with a bit of reluctance that they share their treasure with the world.

I believe Bob Dylan is one of the greatest poets of all time. I recently discovered his song, "Every Grain of Sand." I think I understand maybe half of it, but I agree with other Dylan fans that this may be one of the greatest songs ever written. I think it's about the universe. I think it's also about the Divine. It's about nature and our place and significance and things like that. But, even when poets are asked to explain their own creations, it's often difficult for them to explain what they were trying to say.

The Christian Scriptures were written over a period of 1600 years. It is a record of people struggling to understand God. Many of them were prophets and poets. Along with the authors of the Bible, there are probably hundreds of thousands of seekers that have written about their quest to understand God and the Universe and how it all works together. They spoke in different languages and used different methods, but the way to recognize a poet or a prophet is that they don't come to definite conclusions. When someone writes to a definite conclusion, we can be certain that they settled for an elementary understanding of things and they probably were not a prophet or poet. Poets and prophets are searching for something deeper—something more Divine.

In some ways, I am trying to put language to the things I am discovering. In many ways, I try to share this with other people, hoping they will find words for the things that they are thinking. That's a lot of what connection, one of our deepest needs is about. We want to hear a song or read a book that resonates with us. That part of us that has an inclination that things can be understood is what keeps us scrolling and reading and listening to music. But, the other part of us has an inclination that some things are very hard to describe. We need the poets and prophets because some things only get muddied when we try to define them. They can wrestle with thoughts and ideas without having to *wrangle* them into a belief or a system.

To me, love songs are when a poet attempts to put something into words that cannot adequately be described with words. In interviews, they say a lot of things like "It's like … " or "It reminds me of … " People often get mad at them because they seem elusive and unclear. But they are trying to describe something deeper and more mysterious than their language can define. People want to nail down the prophets of the Bible to be some kind of fortune tellers, but they were really just people trying to put into words what they were discovering when they went deeper—when they went inside.

In the introduction, I mentioned the idea of "sinking" to get closer to the Divine. It comes from the popular Bible verse that we usually interpret "*Be still* and know that I am God."[9] When we "cease striving" or "be still," we are able to *sink* into the mysteries that are deeper and more ancient than our words can adequately describe. In my book, *The Tea Shop,* I talk about Van Morrison's song, where he encourages us to *float* "Into the Mystic." Many times, the conversation with mystics is stalled by the statement, "It's very hard to describe." Most contemplatives I know talk about *going inside,* but don't ask them for a formula! It's just a *sinking,* or a *drifting* that is hard to turn into a formula or prescription or even a belief.

If our practices can be succinctly described, we will remain in the kiddie pool of the spiritual world. But when we can *sink,* we can discover more of the depths of the creator and this divine creation. When we allow ourselves to *float,* we find not a slippery slope but a current of understanding that we may not be able to describe, but we will know much more deeply. We can experience more of the vastness of this mysterious, mystical, and limitless journey when we let the prophets

---

9   Psalms 46:10

and poets lead us there with their colorful versions of "It's kind of like this … "

Even though it's hard to go deeper with the prophets and poets, it's not a waste of time. When we ponder words and thoughts that are hard to wrangle, it deepens our understanding of the things that really matter. History shows that most new discoveries and new understanding comes from these mystical people that dare to imagine what couldn't be described at the time. We found words for all their imaginations, but in many ways when we did, it put limits on them. We built walls around their expanding ideas and tamed them.

It's time to be wild again. Take a prophet or poet on the journey and *float* out into the mystic. Dive deep into the mysteries of life and let yourself *sink* long enough to *know* what can only be imagined, not defined. Take a step out into the desert with those that have ventured there and find mystery and paradox and nuance, not certainty and doctrine.

The Poets and the Prophets

by Karl Forehand

The poets and the prophets,
    don't know anything for sure.
They know what they feel inside,
    and that it's possibly a cure.

The poets and the prophets,
    are never sure that they are right.
They just are very thoughtful,
    and we often think they might.

The poets and the prophets,
    never begged to have the stage.
They just knew they long to tell,
    what they saw as they turned the page.

The poets and the prophets,
    lead us forward with their thoughts.
They don't always know the way,
    but they say it at great cost.

The poets and the prophets,
    might feel the weight of our strife.
They just keep sharing their hearts—
    It's their hearts that bring us life.

BEING WITH COMMUNITY

After attending church for roughly 25 years, we took some time off. We stepped out of regular church attendance and membership in an organization to just be together as a couple on Sunday. We don't attend any of the activities that are hosted by organizational churches. One reason is because much of what we get there is easy to find electronically, but we have also been through a lot of church trauma and just about everything in those circles triggers us in some way. We are working on that trauma, but it makes it difficult to heal when you keep re-injuring the same spots.

When we try to discuss this with people in the church, we always get the same response. In one way or another, people tell us we need community. Sometimes it is followed by shaming statements like "You should be in a church" or "Just come on home—this is your home" or something like that. I believe we need community, but is the modern-day, organizational church the place to find it?

I ask this question because the typical church experience goes something like this. We show up on Sunday and send the kids off to Sunday School. We stop by the coffee shop, in church, to get a quick boost. Usually, we talk briefly with a couple of people. I notice that most people talk to the same few people every week except when some outgoing person introduces them to someone else. When it's time, we are ushered into a climate-controlled auditorium where we say hi to the same people we saw last week before making ourselves ready for the show that we see every week. I say "show" because if it is planned, practiced, and performed pretty much the same way every time. There are special shows like Christmas and Easter, but they are also versions of the show. There are variations to the message and the songs; but most things are what we expect. There is one speaker and the rest of us listen. After the service, we visit outside for a few minutes mostly with the same people each week.

Later in the week, we may attend an alternate service or a discipleship class. But this is also taught by one person while the rest of us listen. Sometimes churches opt for small groups in people's homes. This is probably the part of organized religion that comes closest to the community that we could probably hope for. The rest of church life in modern-day America is just a thing we attend once a week that makes us feel a little better until we get back to work on Monday morning. We spend a tremendous amount of money to put on the best show in town so that other people will come to our show and identify with us, but I would suggest that it falls way short of community. And if small groups in our home are like real communities, why don't we start there instead of going through all that other stuff before coming back "home" to the real community (that actually is in our community)?

I am pretty sure that at least the need for connection is wired into our brain. We inherently know that we need it, even if we identify as an introvert. I can honestly say that I have found community within organized religion at times, mostly in small towns. As a pastor, I felt like I had a community because someone always talked to me. I just had to stand at the door as they went out and at least one other person told me of my worth on the way out. The thing I didn't have was deep friendships. I thought I did, but I found out how shallow those relationships were when I changed some of my beliefs or stopped attending that church. In most cases, they stopped talking to me—in other cases, I wished they would have!

Just because we are somewhat tribal does not mean that we have true community in our churches. Just because we have a common hatred for other groups doesn't make us intimate. Common enemy intimacy is counterfeit culture and does nothing substantiate our claim of community. Many times, we rally around the same political opponents or recite the same creeds and think we're fully engaged in the family, when in fact true community is much more than that. Real community means being fully open to other ideas and fully accepting of all people regardless of their religious or political beliefs or sexual orientation. In my opinion a true community would not only be fully accepting of Baptists, Catholics, and Methodists, but also homosexuals, Muslims, Hindus and atheists (just to mention a few).

But, community is even more than that. The community that I imagine is a place where we trust each other enough to share all our wounds and all our struggles. When we do this, we should find nothing but compassion, seasoned with grace, love and mercy! Organized religion has typically not been characterized by vulnerability in my experience. Organizations have a tough time with intimacy and love. It's not that they don't have that intention, but they are not structured with enough time to allow for that type of closeness. If it's going to happen, it happens on the edges of the organization with people committed to honest, vulnerable experiences and a dedication to be companions on your journey.

The truth about community is that we can find it anywhere. It might be in a church, but It also might be at a bar, or a gym or even sometimes within our actual families. Community is experienced while we are in a relationship. Deep, vulnerable relationships that are honest and daring and persistent build communities wherever they are. It may be the way of Christ that is being lived out, but the location of that community is almost irrelevant. It is the willingness to be vulnerable and open and trusting that builds a foundation for connection. And it is things like acceptance and openness and forgiveness that lays the cornerstones of community upon the bedrock of sacrificial love. The living stones of the community are usually known to be loving, forgiving and non-judgmental. The mortar that holds them together is not their denomination, or political persuasion or even their religious beliefs. It is their commitment to each other, regardless of their uniqueness, that binds them together.

How can I get involved in a community?

Realize You Have Something To Give

Every time I join a community, I try to tell them "I'm a little slow out of the gate." The reason I feel this way is because I've discovered it is unfruitful to just try to do what they expect me to do. In the past, I would have scurried around doing everything because then they wouldn't reject me or kick me out of the club. Usually, this happened at work where I eventually got roped into something that I was doing well that wasn't necessarily the best fit for who I am.

Now, it's different. It takes a little longer, I slowly try to see how the things that I am match the realities of the job and I strive to do the things that are genuinely me and match those to the needs of the group. If I can discover these matches during the interview, I make better promises and they know what to expect. To do this, I must know who I am and what I have to offer. Sure, I can learn new skills, but the way of my being must match the truth of my being or my journey is going to be much more painful.

Growing up, I wore a lot of hand-me-down clothes. When I started earning my own money, one of the first things I bought was clothes. Often, I was so desperate to have something new that I didn't try it on to see if it fit. Inherit in this process is being sure of what is best for me and the community and being able to say "no" to the things that don't fit well. Not only do I need to be confident to step into the arena, but I also must know who I am and say no to outfits (so to speak) that are not right for me.

The need for community is real. Analogies and illustrations always fall short, so let me just say the following about giving ourselves to the group. It is important to know who we are and what we must give, but almost as important is to know who we are giving it to. Is the group compatible with my needs as much as they need me to increase their numbers? Can they feed and nourish my soul or are they likely to exhaust and drain my resources for the needs of the group?

Realize You Have Something To Say

Online communication played a vital role in the COVID-19 crisis that is currently still happening as I am writing this. People began forming discussion groups and meeting online through the different advances in technology. It was a sight to see and eventually turned into a storm of noise at times, even though it was very helpful. One common reaction of people was to silence themselves when they didn't think what they had to say was valid. Even when I was interviewing someone for a podcast, they would often throttle themselves because they didn't want to "say too much" or "go on-and-on."

Too many of us lost our voices at various times in our lives. We were told that our ideas were stupid or only the most eloquent were to speak for the rest of us. At other times, in these online groups, I would ask for everyone's opinions. Often, after a little stammering, we would receive the wildest, most innovative thoughts from someone who otherwise wouldn't have spoken. I must believe that what I think and what I feel is important because it is what I think and feel. That matters.

Bullies of the past have silenced the voices that disagreed with them, but it's time now for all voices to be heard. As we mature and grow into ourselves and find our voice, we realize we are not surrounded by our parents nor do we have to live in the past. We are allowed to speak even when we are not spoken to. Too many women and introverts and marginalized people have kept silent or been silenced by power brokers. If we are going to experience the community we want, all voices must be heard.

My part in this struggle seems to be realizing that what I have to say is worth hearing. I must believe that my song is worth singing. Even though the people that like control get uneasy, it's still my obligation to speak my truth. My question may concern a frightened leader, but that says more about them than it does about me. If I speak from my heart and know who I am, to truly be in the community is to speak just like I listen.

Realize You Have Much To Gain

One of the things about us introverts is that we falsely believe or can be lulled into believing that we don't really need anyone. Deep down, we know it's not true but most of the time, we simply are happy just being by ourselves and doing our own thing. Why would we want to join a community? I am assuming that extroverts have an issue with not knowing how to just be in silence or solitude. We all have our issues. We all face challenges when it comes to community. But, all of us gain something from connection with others. As I said before, it's wired into our brains—we need connection and that usually happens in community. I am not qualified to explain to you exactly what it is. But what I know from experience and from counsel is that we profit from genuine, vulnerable, nurturing communities like what happens when we feed ourselves with the right nutrition. We need not only to stay alive, but we also can thrive.

We are currently practicing what has become known as *social distancing* because of the current crisis in the United States and Missouri. It mostly means that we don't go to work, and we try to stay at home most of the time. We go out about every 5 days and get some of the perishable groceries. We occasionally go out for other necessities. Every time we go out, we risk catching the virus, but we risk it because we know that unless we put food into our body on a regular basis we will suffer, get sick and eventually die. On top of that, I learned that putting the best food into my body gives me the best chance of thriving here on earth.

Even if we feel afraid or vulnerable to be in community, it is necessary for our physical, emotional and spiritual health. Without what we gain from the community, we will suffer and eventually wither without taking in that nutrition that we gain from every meal. Sure, there's a bit of waste involved and sure some things don't taste exactly right, but we must learn what we gain from the community and not feel guilty when it's time to eat.

Again, I'm not stressing that you find your community inside a church. If organized religion keeps you alive and vibrant, do what works for you. But realize community can come from any place where you find sacrificial, self-giving love. Also, as I said before, it helps to be where you are and know who you are but realize you may be on a journey to a new community with new friends and new family members. Don't sacrifice your soul for the community, simply give and receive and speak your truth.

Being in community is central to your journey. I hope you make it a priority.

Being in Community

by Karl Forehand

Community is good, I think it is true,
    not sure I care where I find it.
They say 'come' to church, I say 'no, that hurts,'
    For me, it just doesn't work.

Connection is good, I know it is true,
    it seems to be part of our wiring.
We need to ways to give, we reach out to live,
    For me, it's not just suggestive.

People are good, I know it is true,
    We can't just hide out forever.
The way to be sure, and be part of the cure,
    For us, is to keep our hearts pure.

BEING WITH NATURE

"In every walk in with nature one receives far more than he seeks.
JOHN MUIR[10]

When I was younger, my friend and I would shoot birds out of the trees. After night church, me and the pastor's son would shine flashlights up into the trees and shoot the birds with our pellet guns. It pales in comparison to what we pay for others to do in factory farms these days, but it was still cruel! Before I had a pellet gun, I burned ants on the sidewalk with a magnifying glass. It was just part of being a typical kid in the time and place that I grew up. I've given up hunting all together, but there is a part of me (even as a vegan), that still respects hunting for food.

So, given my past, it surprised me the other day when I was warming up my car and listening to a bird singing. It was most likely the same type of bird that I pelted with lead not that many years ago. I realized that this bird is the first thing I hear when I awake every morning. It is most likely a robin, because this pair have been building a nest about 10 feet from our bedroom window for the past few years. The first year, we watched them build the nest and now they come back every year to tidy up and get ready for the new arrivals. It is exciting, and we look forward to it every year. It's not only one of the signs of Spring, but it's an example of new life! I like to think they trust us, but we know they are mostly just doing their thing and trying not to get eaten by another animal.

---

10 https://wisdomquotes.com/nature-quotes/

The rabbits and squirrels are a little more elusive. Occasionally, we see the squirrels scamper across the porch or chase each other up a tree. The bunnies move around and do not let us see them too often, but we appreciate it when they do. There is a family of foxes in town, the occasional snake and the moles that migrate around just below the surface. In our area, it would be easy to spot deer, wild turkeys, racoons, opossums, and coyotes.

The main thing I miss about hunting is sitting in a tree stand in the silence and stillness of the very early morning. As the sun would creep up to the horizon, the animals would make themselves known. Before the white noise of civilization rang out, the birds began their singing. As light began to emerge, the creatures that roamed the land began moving. Some were gathering food, some were coming home from the night's hunt, and others took flight from their perch just above my head.

There is great diversity in nature, but there also seems to be a steady rhythm. It is almost like a drumbeat—it is persistent and predictable. Nature doesn't have to be coerced into living. It simply follows an ancient path that it authentically and intuitively knows. Everything I observe in nature has this in common: every part seems to know what it is and where it is. Nature doesn't long to be somewhere else or to be something else. It is in session with the present and at peace with its identity. These two things are what I long for—presence and authenticity.

When the robin's nest was dislodged last year, we helped them re-establish it. But even before we were able to help, they had already begun rebuilding. Nature reacts to disturbances and changes, but not in panic or with despair. It simply alters its course or adapts to the change presented. The fact that we have a dog drove the moles out of our yard, but I'm sure they simply relocated. The rabbits moved nearby for the same reason. I'm mindful that everything I do on my property affects the parts of nature that are there. But nature doesn't seem to get angry or depressed. It seems to adjust its course without missing much of a beat. Do I always respond this well to change? When my ecosystem gets challenged, do I simply adjust with such certainty?

Another interesting aspect of nature to ponder is the soil. In the dirt and clay and sand that lays beneath my feet are all the nutrients for most living things on this planet. As plants grow down into this "earth," they draw up into them the vital minerals and vitamins that they need. Calcium, Zinc, Iron, Magnesium, and other minerals are all there ready to be extracted and used by all of creation. The amino acids that form into proteins, the carbohydrates that break into energy and the phytonutrients that provide fuel and function to most everything here, is found in this soil. But how does it get there?

This question led me to my compost pile. I keep a container near my back door. It is where we discard all our plant scraps including peelings, expiring fruits and vegetables and anything plant-based that we can't use any more. It reduces our trash load and eventually gets moved to an upside-down bucket that serves as our compost pile. I mix in some leaves and yard waste and even our coffee grinds and over time, the waste becomes something useful—dark rich, compost that feeds the soil. It's a small model of what happens naturally all over the world. When things die, they are acted upon by nature and repurposed into life giving forms. You might call it the circle of life, but to me it seems like one big choreographed dance.

To observe nature closely is to understand this parade of life through all its being born and dying and we briefly catch a glimpse of how death leads to resurrection and resurrection to new life. I often resist change, but change is not only probable, it's imminent! Change will happen naturally, and nature is only delayed briefly by the disruptions.

Recently I started sprouting again. I buy sprouting seeds from the internet that are made of broccoli, radishes, clover and alfalfa. It is called "broccoli and friends." I put some seeds in a jar and keep them wet for a few days, and like magic it turns into these little tiny plants that are chocked full of nutrition. When I watch this happen, I see the Divine contained in that little seed that quickly becomes a highly nutritious (and very tasty) sprout. What I know from research is that all the potential for that entire plant is found in that tiny little seed. As scientists probe deeper into molecules, they find this majesty deep within all things.

To be honest, I wrestle with whether a holy being would require worship. I just don't see God or the Creator or Source being that needy. I think if any being is self-assured, I think it would be the one that created all this. Most of nature doesn't wait for approval before it proceeds. Only those that we domesticate and tame seem to have the same delusions as us. The plants and animals don't have to have praise to continue doing what they do. My assumption is that the creator of these beings simply IS and that is enough. If the accounts are right, the revelations of God reveal him to say "I am" several times. To exist is not only what matters, but it is enough.

So, nature brings me back to a simpler and richer mode of existence. It reminds me that being where I am and who I am is not only enough, it is also magical and mystical and teaming with life, death, resurrection and then new life once again. As I start another new day, I have heard the bird sing. His song leads me out into the yard where I catch a glimpse of one of the creatures doing its thing. I peer down at the soil, and just for a moment, my mind can almost comprehend the universal and cataclysmic dance of the universe. That's where I find humility these days—that's where I find truth—it's where I draw energy—it's where I find life!

Being with Nature

by Karl Forehand

I love being out with nature,
    I love to be out in the air.
I love to feel the earth in my footsteps,
    I love to be somewhere out there.

I love to see animals frolic,
    I love to hear birds sing their songs.
I love to talk walks in the outside,
    I really don't care if it's long.

I love to image a drumbeat,
    That gives all the creatures their cue.
It really is more of a heartbeat
    That wakes them up with the dew.

It seems that there's not much complaining,
    They certainly know who they are.
It enough to just to do what they usually do
    And to be in the place where they are.

BEING WITH PAIN

Recently one of my friends shared how she has practiced yoga for 99 days straight. Many people congratulated her, but I didn't hear anyone that said, "Me too." Why? Because exercise, getting in shape and creating healthy habits is hard. We take a long walk and our bodies seem to scream out warnings that even a little bit of exercise is way more than we are accustomed to. When I haven't done yoga, I can feel emotions releasing from my body when I stretch and make space. It's painful physically and even emotionally to intentionally begin a new practice when we have been negligent.

Everyone knows that, even after a few days, our bodies will begin to adjust to the new routine and become stronger so that we don't feel as much pain even with more involved practices. Every day, we will be able to walk further or lift more or breath better. But, there's the pain! It's always going to be painful first.

We also find pain when we try to address emotional, spiritual and trauma-based issues in our lives. To survive, we often bury our struggles rather than deal with them. At the point of the wounding, we either didn't know how to deal with them or we didn't feel like we were able to endure the pain involved with confronting issues. Sometimes even good things we could have done get buried because they seem painful or they don't fit into our current environment and we avoid doing what we know we could, because the reward seems less than the effort of pain of moving forward.

For many years, I could barely lead a silent prayer without passing out. I flunked a speech in college because I forgot the second half of it and I almost passed out right there in front of the class. I wasn't even sure what I was afraid of, but it was extremely painful. It was sort of like climbing a mountain with no clothes on. When I was forced to speak, I would finish the endeavor exhausted and wrung out emotionally—it at least felt extremely painful to speak publicly, so I avoided it like the plague until I couldn't anymore. Coming out of this cycle was extremely painful. My terror of public speaking was rooted deep inside me and had created an atrophy that would take years to reverse.

In college, I learned about pleasure and pain. They told me that some of our primary wiring in our brain is that we avoid things we perceive to be painful and seek after things we believe to provide pleasure[11] There is no doubt what we think will bring us pleasure and what we fear will be painful is often skewed. In my experience, it is often deeply distorted. Never-the-less, pain and pleasure are great motivators. We go to unbelievable lengths to avoid and pursue what we think will benefit. All this makes me thankful for mindfulness in my current practices, because at the least I can hopefully sort through all this confusion a little more effectively.

So, what options do we have to deal with the pain?

The most obvious option and one I'm most familiar with is *quitting*. I can stop exercising because it is painful hoping I'll be more motivated later. Maybe there will be a better option or some piece of equipment that is somehow easier. I can withdraw from a relationship because it's painful to have these discussions. Maybe there's some secret I haven't discovered yet. I can quit my job because surely there's a better

---

11 https://en.wikipedia.org/wiki/Pain_and_pleasure

company out there. Granted, there are times to quit, but most times quitting only delays the pain until the next situation reminds us, we did not deal with the root issue.

My brothers and I played a lot of organized sports as kids. My parents never made us play anything, but my dad had one simple rule: *If you sign up for the team, you cannot quit.* He knew that after we got through the initial pain of getting in shape that we would be able to reap all the positive benefits of being on the team. This model would be deeply tested in high school when I experienced two-a-day football practices.

This in no way means that we shouldn't ever exit a relationship that is abusive or a situation that is producing trauma for us. There are things that we should quit, but we cannot quit everything that is hard. We can't stop going to counseling because it involves encountering things that are difficult. We can't keep quitting everything and expect to move forward. We may need to halt a relationship, but then face the pain of restoring our well-being. There is not any gentle slide down to joy and happiness. It's most always hard, painful work that requires persistence and patience.

The second way we often try to deal with pain is through *numbing*. I can hear the religious elites warming up the choir. We love to criticize alcohol and drug abuse. There is no doubt that these are issues in society, but there are many ways we anesthetize our pain instead of dealing with it including prescription drugs. People even use religion to numb the pain that they don't want to face. Spiritual bypassing is when we use religious phrases and practices to bypass encountering things that might be painful. Activities, religion, hobbies, vacations, work, and various vices can all be things that help us forget about the pain. They all promise to take away the pain, but they just mask it for a while and sometimes drive it deeper within us. If we continue to numb the pain, the sure reality is that we will see it again later when it comes out sideways.

I was convinced I could bury the painful rejection I felt at various times in my life. Over the years I continued to numb that pain and try to pretend that it wasn't there. Occasionally, it would cause me to act out in various ways. I would blow up for no reason or react in unusual ways to small things. After apologizing, I returned to my life and continued to use the business of my life to numb the pain of rejection. Then, one weekend, it all came rushing out in one of the most bizarre and painful weekends of my life. It almost ended my marriage and certainly derailed my career for some time. Numbing the pain never really reduces or solves the problem of pain. Emotional pain does not get better on its own, so numbing agents only help temporarily and make the problem worse.

The only real way to deal with pain in our life is to *lean into it*. Just like I had to keep exercising to get in shape, getting in emotional shape often requires facing some things that are painful and stepping into them. Again, this doesn't mean staying in abusive situations; but it may mean facing the abuser or reporting them or facing what we feel deep down about this abuse. Many of us stay in the situation and escape emotionally or just keep ourselves busy enough where we don't think about it.

As I briefly mentioned, mindfulness has been a helpful practice for me. Some people think of practices like this as escaping because they imagine it's an escape to some peaceful meadow somewhere. Certainly, yoga and meditation and things like this can provide relaxation and escape, but what they most promote are presence and taking on the role of an observer. Sometimes this journey is blissful, but occasionally it is deeply painful and troubling. When we can be with ourselves and observe what is beneath the service, we can step into what gives us joy AND what deeply troubles us. When we are able to observe instead of judging or shaming or avoiding, we can approach this necessary space with compassion.

Eventually, I would lean into the pain of past rejection. It was a week of deep work that changed my life. I would describe it as *shadow work* and *focusing* that helped me face the inner child and inner critic and all emotional things that I had stored in my body. Our bodies are amazing vehicles that tie the physical, spiritual and emotional together. The body doesn't take kindly to things stored within that are not helpful and healthy to store there. We can ignore those things for a while, but we will see them again and they may be behaving badly when they return.

Leaning into our pain not only helps us solve our issues, it also helps us *learn* about them. Some things we can't solve magically and some of them, if understood, can become strengths instead of weaknesses. That is probably a whole other book that someone has already written but suffice to say that we can learn by being an observer. When we lean in and bring fresh air to our pain, it begins to heal, and it loses its control over us. Even though we become more aware, it is not our focus anymore. It's just a part of us that we know better.

Some pain is okay. It's okay to be sad about some things. Feeling the weight of things sometimes can be helpful, if the empathy and compassion we feel extends to all people, including ourselves. Pain is an early warning sign that something is wrong. It needs our attention and that's really the point of all this. Lean in and experience the pain, observe it. The intensity will lesson over time and then we'll understand its purpose and design.

Being with Pain

by Karl Forehand

The first step may seem like it's daunting
    To take it seems almost too massive.
But then we lean in, and then and again,
    We learn there's no progress that's passive.

BEING WITH SOLITUDE

> *"Knowing how to be solitary is central to the art of loving. When we can be alone, we can be with others without using them as a means for escape."*
>
> ANONYMOUS

As I discussed earlier, we are currently experiencing the COVID-19 pandemic. It has required us to practice what is known as *social distancing*. Americans seem to resist anything that we believe limits our freedom. Even when the limitations can save our life, we like to think we know what is best for us (even when we have very little information to base those decisions upon). I suppose most people reading this will remember the crisis and will be able to identify with one view of the other of this isolation that was required of us, either by choice or by force.

There is a part of me that believes that some people like isolation better than others. I have always identified as an introvert, but I also seem to crave approval and acceptance. I am like a hermit in a cave that occasionally must come out and say, "What do you think of this?" I suppose many writers and artists feel that way. We enjoy the solitude, but occasionally we crave that someone would enjoy what we've created. It's primarily for us, but we also have secondary desires to see it affect someone else.

The situation we are in has me thinking about the difference between solitude and isolation. Is there a difference and does it even make any difference whether I am an introvert or not? Like most things, I'm not disciplined enough to do a lot of research, I would rather just tell you about what I am inclined towards. I'd rather just let people correct me later and try to remember to thank them and not take it personally.

Isolation seems to bear with it the negative image of being pushed away or running away. By its nature, it seems to indicate that we are not being allowed to do something or we are avoiding something we should or could be doing. In its simplest forms, maybe it's not our primary choice, but something we were coerced into or led to by our poor choices. Solitude seems to be a much better option. Even though technically it is similar, the reviews and results seem to be much more positive.

Solitude seems to be a positive choice we make. It is moving toward rather than running away from something. It is when we step back and breathe and go inward. In solitude, we disconnect to the outside and connect to the internal. It is an attitude or mindset that seems to spark our creativity and inner strength. It helps us to know ourselves better and map our lives in an authentic way. Maybe it is an attitude—maybe it is a mindset—maybe it is a purpose toward intentionally living this way. All I know is that I crave it these days. Even if I am being forced, I find fulfillment in solitude.

It is true that we need connection and we seemed to be hard-wired for it. But, in our modern communities, we seem to always be doing. We convince ourselves that the road to fulfillment is in always having something to accomplish. The to-do list is our manifesto, and, in the process, we forget who we are. And, in response to our need for connection, our religion can become just *being with people;* but because we are not authentic and grounded, we never really connect, and we return to our isolation feeling defeated. My hunch is that if we would realize we need solitude and apply it effectively, we would better be able to navigate our lives with authenticity and strength, instead of recklessly accumulating friends and accomplishments for no real gain.

I remember learning about contemplative prayer and discovering that it ideally requires at least 20 minutes of silence. When we are in a crowd, a minute of silence can seem like an eternity. *Dead air* on a podcast or a new program can be frightening to those that are managing it. We live in societies that are chocked full of activity. Our minds are constantly occupied with tasks; and, if we are not engaged in conversation, we seem to require alternate stimulation. Our minds race furiously through the day, up until the moment we collapse in exhaustion at the end of the day.

This began to change for me when I attended a quietness retreat. The location was a peaceful retreat center in the middle of a busy metropolitan area. The whole process only took a few hours, but it was divided into five sessions of 20 minutes each. Remember, this was when I barely believed, how could I sit in stillness for one 20-minute session, much less five of them. The host coached us on the process and invited us to let go of all the activity in our minds and just be still.

During the first session, my mind was still racing, and it did seem like an eternity. The second session seemed to go a little quicker, but I still wondered whether I was accomplishing anything. Somewhere during the middle session, I remembered that I did not need to accomplish anything, and I started to just *be* there. The final two sessions seemed more like falling asleep and waking up than meditating or praying. I couldn't really explain what I received, but I knew that it was good.

Something within me realized there is a knowing within me that is hard to describe and is hard to access outside of solitude. At the same time, I was working at a job that required me to go to bed earlier at night and arise sooner in the morning. Mindfulness and solitude help me fall asleep almost instantly at night, but also has a different effect on me in the morning. As I sat in my recliner in the early morning, I seldom had the inclination to set an intention; rather, I was simply being in solitude before the cares of the world could overtake me. I found that this experience of solitude in the morning helped bring me into focus and gave me more strength and wisdom for the day.

Many worry that mindfulness and solitude are an escape from reality. I find the opposite to be true. For me, it is putting off the falseness of my world and going inward to find what is true and worthy. I find a knowing within that seems much more ancient. I learn of the invincible preciousness that is inside me. Although it seems vulnerable at the time, and I must face both the darkness and the light, I feel like my eyes are wide open and I am consciously compassionate and aware of all these things.

There are many labels we might attach to this thing called solitude, but the best label I can determine is *being*. It is authentically and intentionally being where I am and who I am long enough to nod "yes" to the Universe and the Divine and proceed with my life.

I hope this pandemic helps us to be more compassionate toward each other. Right now, it is hard to see whether that is happening or not. Currently people are arguing whether they should abstain from church services. Most agree that we should for the public's safety, but there are some that fear this might infringe upon their rights to do what they please. Others would argue that whether you are in a building does not affect your ability to commune with God and they wonder why all the fuss. Sometimes, you must be creative.

But as people miss their physical communities of religion, work and play, I'm sure many doubts have arisen. What if some of these things don't return to normal. And, what if some of these things were not normal to begin with. I now believe we only know the answer to questions like this when we go inside. One of the most important questions initiated by the pandemic may be, "What is really important?" And, then the subsequent question may be, "What is not?"

When we are traveling along at the speed of life, it's hard to determine what is essential and what is simply demanded by our circumstances. The tyranny of the urgent shouts down any reasoning that would slow it down from getting where it's going (even if it doesn't know for sure where it is headed at the time).

We have been given an opportunity. We can take this forced isolation to be intentional and experience some real solitude. Possibly, we could at least be without remorse that we are neglecting the to-do list. Because there is less urgency, we can throw off the shackles of its tyranny. We can listen and observe without any objective. And, maybe we will discover there is something we have been searching or longing for that we couldn't put into words. Maybe we will hear and respond to understanding of what really is important and what is not. Possibly, we will isolate ourselves more often and find the strength in solitude to be where we are and who we are more often.

Being with Solitude

by Karl Forehand

Solitude seems like a sentence
    We should earnestly try to avoid.
But really, it's more like a gift that we get
    That we simply can learn to enjoy.

BEING WITH UNCERTAINTY

"I have never had clarity; what I have always had is trust."
MOTHER TERESA[12]

As we are still in the middle of a pandemic known as COVID-19, I have been off work for a few weeks and they were calling to let me know that it's going to be at least another week before we go back to work. I'm also waiting for my deployment on a nuclear job in June and, so far, it's still in the works. The stimulus money from the government arrived in my account today, but the online banking app isn't working so I don't know for sure if my unemployment check made it into the account. I've never taken unemployment, so this is new to me. To make a long story short, there seems to be a lot of uncertainty in my life.

My natural response to this uncertainty is to engage in getting my world a little more organized. I can make some phone calls, get some reassurances and study up on everything so I know more concretely what to expect. If there is one thing I have learned from this pandemic, it is that nothing is for certain. What we did yesterday might not be what we're doing tomorrow. Or, we may be doing the same things for 3 weeks straight. The best laid plans may or may not be realized in times like these—and there are always times like these eventually.

Many of us applied our need for certainty to religion. If we can be sure of some things, we imagine we should be sure of most things.

---

[12] https://quotefancy.com/quote/869450/Mother-Teresa-I-have-never-had-clarity-what-I-have-always-had-is-trust-So-I-will-pray

The more that we can nail things down, the more secure we will feel. At least that is what we think.

Certainty is a lot like a drug. That feeling of being right and being able to predict what will happen gives us a rush of superiority and security. We also long for other people to affirm and confirm our assumptions. We call them beliefs or truths and hope that others will confirm them and take away the anxiety we feel when those thoughts are questioned. Because of our addiction to this certainty and the illusion that we need it, when someone dares to take it away, we become quite irrational.

When certainty was important to me, I was anything but at rest. Opposing views to what I was certain about were perceived as personal attacks. In social media circles, you can tell people that have a lot of certainty about their beliefs. They react very strongly, almost irrationally, to anyone that questions what they believe to be true. Often, simple questions are answered with vicious, character assaults or demeaning rhetoric. I have been on both ends of those conversations. Because I saw questions about my views as personal attacks, I spent hours researching the "right answers" and usually believed I had them. Often, for religious people, the way, truth and life of Jesus is believed to be something each group believes they possess inside of their certainty. If it's that sacred, it must be defended!

At some point, I realized I had to release what was unsustainable. From the time my mentor pastor told me I needed to decide how I felt about whether Jesus was peccable or impeccable, I had been on a quest to become as certain as I could about as many of my beliefs as I was able. And, it was exhausting and often my research only raised more questions, which left me feeling more vulnerable. At some point, I just had to acknowledge that I might be wrong about some things and maybe I do not know as much as I think or do; or maybe, gasp... none of it is right! In one sense, this seemed like giving up, but the more steps I took, I realized it was really like a significant journey in a desert of understanding. I had a sense that I was discovering what faith was about—not unbridled certainty, but something like what Mother Teresa was talking about. Not clarity, but trust!

A person that was helpful in this journey for me was Peter Enns. In his book, *The Sin of Certainty,* he explains:

> "When we reach the point where things simply make no sense, when our thinking about God and life no longer line up, when any sense of certainty is gone, and when we can find no reason to trust God but we still do, well that is what trust looks like at its brightest—when all else is dark."

To me, being with uncertainty is kind of like that. When we detach from these false assumptions that we need certainty, we can be present with our presence within and discover things we were never able to see. Contrary to what people told us, these are not dangerous things—they are not evil things—they are the most authentic things that we can now be aware of. As Enns describes, this is what trust looks like at its brightest.

In a way, I regret that I spent so much time in my confined little world of certainty. I think about the hours I spent defending what I was certain about, mostly because I was afraid that my house of cards would be violated. The house came down eventually anyway—the sweater came unraveled—my belief system went through a thorough reconstruction. I called it defending my faith, but what I was defending wasn't really faith at all—it was certitude. It wasn't trust, it was a mixture of theology and apologetics and a large amount of fear. In retrospect, it wasn't really what I now imagine God would encourage us to do. Now, my only fear is that we could return to different kinds of certainty with a new set of dogma and beliefs—a new creed or even an ancient one to defend. I don't think its new beliefs necessarily that were the problem. I think it's our attitude toward those beliefs that held us back.

As I move forward, I hold my beliefs loosely. I try to use language like, "this is how I see it at this point in my journey." And, often, I ask questions of others more than espousing what I believe. What I believe is in such a state of development, that I hesitate to chisel anything into stone. You would think that would make me uneasy. Let's just say that it would have a few years ago. But I have learned to be where I am and to be who I am. Hopefully, for the rest of my life, I will be a guy on a journey.

At the current moment, I find myself outside the walls of organized religion. I don't feel like I'm suffering. I have peace on most days, and I feel like I'm moving toward something. As I write and discover and discuss, I find that I am learning what Mother Teresa spoke of—I'm learning to trust. But this trust is not something I've scribed in a document or something that was handed down to me by my ancestors. I realize some of those things can be distorted over time and some of them were never right to begin with. My trust is beginning to be rooted in something deep inside me. There's something ancient about it, and it appears to be untouched by time. Some people call this the inner self or the Divine within.

This invincible preciousness is not the flesh that Apostle Paul talked about. In fact, I think the flesh (or the false self) is what causes us to imagine that we need to have elaborate dogmas and adopt creeds so that we all believe in the same things. This outer ego causes us to fear mystery, paradox and nuance because we can't defend it. For the ego, uncertainty is just a little too risky, but for the authentic self, this mystery lets us know we're on the right journey. Even if it's just our mind that is expanding, the things we need to learn are always going to feel different at first.

Yesterday, my friend (Dr. Paul Fitzgerald), was my companion on a focusing journey to help me identify some blockage I had from past experiences. I was able to sense something in me that felt rejected and needed other's approval. At first, I resisted going on this journey because I had never experienced it as exactly like what I was sensing. I wanted something I could be certain about. But there it is really—we can't go on a journey of discovery where everything is as we expect. That is not a journey! If everything is just like we remember it, we are not discovering anything or learning anything new—we are simply reliving the past.

I pray that you will experience throwing off certainty to go on the journey. It sounds scary to my old friends and they think I am on a slippery slope. But I sense way deep inside me that it is something different. It's more like coming home to something than falling away. It's more like finding my authentic self than losing anything. I don't feel like I'm anywhere close to being complete, but I'm way less empty than I used to be.

Being with Uncertainty

by Karl Forehand

Uncertainty seems like a problem,
    That we anxiously try to avoid.
It seems like we need to resolve it,
    And it faithfully keeps us annoyed.

Doubt also seems like a problem,
    But to faith it is really a friend.
Certainty keeps us from trusting,
    And trust should be the goal in the end.

Journeys can seem like a problem,
    Because they lack a knowing for sure.
But journeys can be to find unknowns
    And arrives at a much better cure.

BEING WITH THE DIVINE

This morning, I was a little upset for a period. I woke up later than usual and poured a cup of coffee. Laura was already up which is unusual. Most mornings, I come to my chair and experience some very quiet, peaceful time alone. Today was different as I needed to take the dog out and Laura was already working. She was talking to herself and listening to a video softly on how to do something with video slides. I put on my earphones and turned up the meditation music. For a moment, I resented that everyone was interrupting my quiet time; but after a few moments, I was able to go within and find that familiar place of rest where I feel God.

During the crisis of COVID-19, millions of people have been confined to their homes and they only go out when they absolutely must for supplies such as food. This isn't like anything we have experienced in our lifetimes. We don't have to go to work, but we can't go out and do things with friends or go on vacation or even go out to eat. All the restaurants are closed and only the essential function businesses are open.

People have argued a lot about various things online, but one thing has become apparent. One of the most important things we need to realize is that we have a deep need for connection. Almost immediately after being confined to our houses, people started organizing online meetings and get-togethers. Connection seems to be hard-wired into our DNA. Even if we call ourselves introverts, we at least occasionally need people that we identify as our people that we can depend on for basic things like love and acceptance.

The other night on a whim, I asked several of the guys online that I have met during the past few years to join me for a video conference. I was a little frustrated with a certain situation and seemed to have lost my peace. These were people that frankly came into my life because I was promoting my book, but later became friends that encourage me. A couple of them have become very close to me in a short amount of time. It was awkward when we first started talking, but then we realized all of us were struggling a little and as we shared our struggles, we felt a connection and somewhat of a peace come over us. Several of them told me they were glad we got together and that we should do it again some time.

In our communities, we want people who will identify with us and sometimes even advocate for us. Occasionally, we hope they will encourage us when we are down and give us some well-timed advice when we are messing up. We want to feel like we are cared for. When we are tired, we hope someone will carry the ball—when we are motivated, we like to have someone that we can give ourselves to. In short, we want someone to love and someone that loves us. We hope this is not just because we are a part of their community, but because they freely choose to do so. As I said before, this community can come from a variety of sources. It doesn't have to be just at church or just in our families or just in a club. It can come from all those places and more; but what we really want is connection, not just community.

Maybe the deepest connection we desire is connection to the Divine. No matter whether we call this God or Creator or Source or something else, this desire to understand and connect with a greater power is something that also seems to be designed into us. Most cultures and peoples from all over the world demonstrate this quest that seems to be a part of them regardless of their history—we seem to be searching to understand and connect with whoever or whatever is calling the shots. Some of us even substitute relationships with powerful or influential people thinking this connection will bring us happiness or success or whatever we are striving for.

This was the nature of my recent struggle. I was trying to connect with the more famous people to give me some credibility or validity to my existence in some way. It's almost subconscious, but I often long to do something significant and I hope to be on the right team. It goes way back in my history and my Spiritual Director helped me visit this part of me the other day and find some resolution. I assume this quest for validation relates somehow to my desire to connect with God.

Connecting with God was complicated in the tradition I grew up in. God was always believed to be way out there somewhere. Since God randomly distributed gifts at whim, it was hard to know what He expected because He was also depicted as a retributive Father that was constantly angry. We would gather in prayer circles and "petition" him for things that most fathers would be glad to bestow on their children. We begged Him for grace and mercy even though the writings about him said He was full of these things.

I must admit, I connected with some people easier at the bar than I was able to connect to "God's people" in "His house." I was able to relate to a wide variety of people in various areas of life but connecting with this God that supposedly loved me seemed elusive and sometimes disheartening. This was made worse by the promises of religious people that this was my most important relationship. Even as a pastor, I felt like I consistently failed to connect with the being that supposedly loves me with all His heart.

What my tradition did not understand or affirm is that God (we'll just use that label for now) is everywhere. Even though the Bible mentions this fact more than once, most groups choose which parts of Scripture to accept and which to ignore. Most traditions pick and choose which parts they will be literal about and which ones they will skip over. When I was in Seminary, they told me that "where you begin is where you end up." Basically, it means that the assumptions we start with when studying anything will greatly influence how we understand it.

Another factor that is like that is the idea that God is in us and, possibly, that God is in all things. This also could be asserted just from a few passages in the New Testament of the Bible. Many world religions believe this also. God is everywhere, because He is Spirit, but he is also in us and in all things. Why would He be everywhere and exclude Himself from the creatures He loves? Along with these ideas, we would naturally assume that if His main attribute is love, He would want to be with those He loves, and He wouldn't hide from those that He cares about. This pandemic has taught us that even humans long to be with the people they love, so why wouldn't His Spirit be in us if that was a possibility. Why would He hide from us—that's not a very good Father.

I now believe this to be true. I believe the Divine is everywhere and, in all things, and the way of connection for us is to go within. In *The Cloud of Unknowing*, the author states, "we can't think our way to God."[13] That's why we've had so much trouble connecting to God. Religious people have tried to imagine God who cannot be adequately imagined. If God is love, we must experience the Divine through things like love and compassion and not through our thinking. When

---

13   Butcher, Carmen Acevedo, *The Cloud of Unknowing: A New Translation*.

we go inside, we can experience everything that God is through sensations, feelings, emotions and listening. You don't really experience a lover by intellectually analyzing them—we know them when we draw close. I don't think we experience God when we think—it's more like we experience Him when we quit thinking and just love.

When we connect with the Divine internally, we find a peace that is hard to explain. We find understanding not through knowledge but through uncertainty. We feel love because we experience it deep within us not when we intellectually can articulate it. We learn to trust something that we cannot explain. I am less able to explain God than I could 20 years ago, but I have experienced Him more deeply than I ever could have imagined. I don't use my intellect to spiritually bypass anymore, but I dive deep into the depths of his love and I perceive Him there. I feel it—I know it—and it heals me from deep inside.

In a previous book, I talked about going into a wooded area and sitting in a clove of trees. After quieting myself and playing some Native American music, I heard and understood the words, "I am a part of this, and this is a part of me." The words connected deeply with where I was mentally and emotionally at the time. It also resonated with my identification with my Native American roots. But the words were not vocal. I didn't even really hear the words—I felt them. It wasn't a matter of logic or reasoning. My mind was not speaking or even hearing the words. My body and soul were feeling it. It's almost as if something ancient came alive inside me. But it didn't float down or blow into me—it seemed like it has always been there. It was more of an awakening and awareness than an invasion. It wasn't hard to welcome this thought because it seemed like it belonged.

That is what my experiences with God are like these days. Every morning and sometimes late at night, I sit in my recliner and meditate for lack of a better word. As I begin to release all the thoughts of the day, I also begin to release my expectations. I would describe it more as a sense of being than doing. Thoughts are when the mind is speaking, but true communion is when the mind is only listening with a simple intention to be and be with the Divine. It is almost like the times when I held Laura's hand and neither of us spoke; but as we were together, we felt as if our hearts were beating together. When I am present with the Divine, I feel many of the things I thought to be true—I feel love and grace and compassion deep within me. It's not that I understand these things better; but I feel them somewhere deep inside me.

Being with the Divine may be less like taking a class and more like taking a break. It is certainly learning to be still and go within without any intentions or expectations. It's not an emotional high that fades away, it is something I experience that was already a part of me. It's less like taking a trip and more like coming home. Being with the Divine in me is loving in its truest sense. I feel the compassion, mercy and grace deeply—it changes me from within.

Being where I am means being where God already is. Being who I am is recognizing that I already possess this love and I become what I have always been—a unique imprint of the Divine.

Being with Divine

by Karl Forehand

Where can I go to find solace?
    Where can I go to find rest?
Where can I go to find peace that abides?
    Where can I be at my best?

Where can I go to find comfort?
    Where can I go to find God?
Where can I go to find wisdom that's true?
    Where can I get what is not?

The peace that abides lies deep inside,
    I can't find it by searching out there.
The wisdom that's ancient and part of myself,
    Is really the kingdom that's near.

BEING WITH THE IGNORANT

Most discoveries I made about sex initially were from my friends. They weren't necessarily qualified to teach me about such things, but at that time, they were the only ones talking about it. "Do you know about … ," they would tease, "No, you probably don't." The journey through the teenage years is one of ignorance and discovery. As a teenager, I thought I knew everything because I was discovering something new every day. At times, I felt like I had been deprived of all things interesting or useful, then a friend would introduce me to something I could have never imagined. I could not even have thought that my parents would possibly know about this new discovery. It helped me be smug for a time, until my ignorance could be revealed the following day on another topic, usually in front of a bunch of people. That's just how it works!

All of us are unaware of some things. I often avoid talking about racial and LGBTQ issues. I believe I have made great strides in these areas recently, but just like my teenage years, I worry that I am ignorant in comparison to others and that will be revealed shortly. Ignorance may have a negative connotation in American culture, but it is just that we are unaware. It would have been so much better to admit in junior high that I wasn't aware of some things instead of pretending to know and shaming myself even worse.

Hopefully, each of us is making discoveries every day. A few days ago, I was able to discover some deep things about myself through some spiritual direction. I love when this happens even though I often resist the hard work required to make these discoveries. I could have gone to the library to learn about sexual things, but I longed for someone to just hand me the information. But, the interesting part of making discoveries and understanding new things is that it changes our relationship to those that are ignorant (unaware) of what we now know. We now know or practice something they may not understand yet. And, like a teenager, we tease them because we want them to acknowledge our newfound understanding, but we don't know how to explain and sometimes they are not interested anyway.

I have noticed that the best way to get a conversation started on social media is to be provocative. Unfortunately, it is also the best way to start a fight. It takes a lot of tact and patience to carefully select words to navigate a social media "discussion." I admire those that can keep their cool and ask questions instead of being accusatory. It's very easy to return to the playground of our youth and begin demeaning and shaming behaviors. It is especially difficult when we are dealing with core beliefs. As we replace our ignorance with knowledge and, hopefully wisdom, we establish beliefs and dogmas that we prefer people don't question. Frantz Fanon, said it this way:

> "Sometimes people hold a core belief that is very strong. When they are presented with evidence that works against that belief, the new evidence cannot be accepted. It would create a feeling that is extremely uncomfortable, called cognitive dissonance. And because it is so important to protect the core belief, they will rationalize, ignore and even deny anything that doesn't fit in with the core belief."

George Burns, the comedian and actor, had a hit song late in life entitled "I Wish I Was 18 Again". I have mixed emotions about this type of thought process. While there are some things I would like to "do over," I don't think I would want to endure the trauma of being a teenager again. But occasionally I daydream about what it would be like to experience those awkward years with the knowledge I have now. What if when I was confronted with something I didn't know, I would simply respond with something reasonable like, "No, I don't know anything about that—please enlighten me!" Then I could employ the Socratic method to go deeper without starting a huge fight or embarrassing myself! Wouldn't that be great—wait, couldn't I apply that to my social media "discussions"?

I'm not ready to throw the baby out with the bathwater. I'm aware (less ignorant) of so many things because I have the internet and social media as resources. I have developed some fabulous relationships online and, of course, made some enemies. I love the fact that my family of origin congregated twice last month online when we hadn't all been together physically in over 10 years. I love that I could bring together four or five psychological experts to talk about the current crisis and then share that conversation with the world. I love that much of the world's knowledge is now at our fingertips. The downside? Not everyone has all the same information or access to it at the same time.

Five years ago, my spiritual beliefs were quite different. I went through what I would call a *de-construction* that was very difficult and often lonely. I delight now that I have found something more beautiful that seems more authentic and I often want to share it with others. But I forget that when I didn't know what I now know, I didn't want anyone to tell me different. It wasn't because I was so proud or anything like that, I was just heavily invested in what I thought to be true. It was part of my livelihood and to admit that I might be wrong, would tear at the foundation of my life. I didn't have time for cognitive dissonance, I needed people to affirm me and support me. I suppose that is common to most of us.

I enjoyed being a preacher for almost two decades. I couldn't lead a silent prayer without passing out in high school. So, preaching was part of my life transformation that I was proud of. I liked convincing people of things I sincerely believed to be true. I had conviction and passion for my part-time profession, but eventually I discovered that preaching is not at all fair. Because the preacher or speaker has prepared in advance, they know what they are going to say and how they are going to say it. Writers could possibly have this advantage too! The audience is not prepared for the subject and is not allowed to prepare a response and usually doesn't have any motivation to do so. It's only in the small groups that we have a greater understanding through discussion and reasonable debate of ideas.

I have always liked listening to good speakers and preachers, but I'm less convinced now that it is an effective way to inform the ignorant. Often, the audience eventually has questions that they want to discuss, but very rarely does the speaker or preacher or blogger have time to dialogue. Not to mention, if this discussion involves core beliefs, the emotions can be a factor that make it worse. I can't take the easy route of "preaching" and condemning anyone that has a dissenting opinion. The best course of action is to take it slow and try to listen as much as I speak.

Another thing that would have been helpful is if I could have admitted that I had fears and insecurities as a teenager. Many of the discussions I long to have is because I want to answer some of the deep questions in my life, but I'm a little unsure about my assumptions and I would love to include some wiser people in the discussion. Why do that online? I think because I hope I can draw some wiser people into the conversation and have a good dialogue about the issue or find pointers to some new information, etc. But, just like a discussion in Junior High, the uninformed (the ignorant) are the first to respond because they are also looking for answers and trying to be significant. If it's accusatory, then I find I am myself defending myself instead of talking about the actual issue.

Maybe, we could all begin the discussion with, "I'm not totally sure about much of this, but here is my assumption." I am tempted just to "like" everything people say and just tell them thanks for contributing, then my ego takes over and I must "set them straight". What we're hoping for is a discussion, but we battle the part of us that wants to always be right. In my deconstruction, I found the most helpful term to be, "Maybe, I'm wrong." At least that adjusts our posture to be less offensive. It doesn't always work, but it helps.

I love the idea that Jesus answered most questions with a question. Much of the time, the questions he received were accusatory in nature. Some of his accusers even went to the level of accusing Him of blasphemy. I find it helpful to ask people questions that ask for clarification of their point or idea instead of accusing them of being wrong. Open ended questions like "Tell me more about why you feel that way" or "What does that mean to you" help diffuse hostile behavior and promotes greater understanding. Too often we let our anxieties lead the discussion instead of our curiosity.

I also like the idea of telling stories. My editor always says, "show, don't tell." It means that it is often better to talk about our experience than our opinion. People want to make up their own minds and our stories help convey what we believe to be important without shaming others into having to respond to our demanding rhetoric. Wm. Paul Young describes our stories as "sacred" and talks about their importance:

> "I don't think we have stories. I think we are stories, and we're stories that I believe will all be told."[14]

Telling a story instead of preaching, reveals a part of us that helps the other person relate instead of demanding that they see our point. The old saying is "They don't care what you know until they know that you care." I think mercy, grace and love should be a part of every conversation, but often we don't even get out of the gate before we are like the teenagers in the locker room cutting each other down. Stories are a way to connect before we start telling what to think.

I still don't care to talk about sex but it's not because it's uncomfortable, it's because it is not an issue I'm wrestling with. I love it—it's great—and being a vegan makes it better. But there are some things that I want to talk about and regardless of what some say, I think we can have some good discussion online. But, just like the schoolyard, it's not going to be easy and we are going to have to be open and teachable if we're going to access this great opportunity that is before us. Online communities and social media cut down the miles and some of the walls that are between us. It doesn't come without its challenges, but neither does a discussion in a hometown coffee shop. Ignorance is not limited to a place or a platform. Unawareness is common to all of us, but it's possible to navigate this challenge if we purpose to do so. Like all of us grew up and became adults, we can also become better at the conversations that are necessary.

---

14   http://wmpaulyoung.com/we-dont-just-have-stories-we-are-stories/

During the pandemic, we came to understand that sometimes our lives depend on having quality conversations. But all conversations are not life or death, and maybe that's the hidden truth in all of this. Maybe, we gain the most by understanding that we're not going to die if we don't prove our point and it's not the end of the world if someone called me a name. Even though we long for honest, genuine dialogue, it's probably always going to be a challenge, but I believe it's still worth the effort.

BEING WITH MY DOG

We adopted Winston into our family when he was about 2 years old about three and a half years ago. Miniature Australian Shepherds are trainable and by nature are herding, community kind of animals. We often say they are smart, but what we mean is that they are about like an above average 3-year old child. I know this because every time I ask him to get me the remote, he just looks at me like I asked him to solve world hunger and then he just lays down on the floor.

Occasionally, I get frustrated with Winston because he does annoying things. He tries to "herd" me by pushing up against my leg. This kind of dog is happiest when everyone in the house is sitting in the living room together. I tell him "One day, you are going to knock me down." Again, he just looks at me and seems to be thinking, "I don't know what you are saying—I want a carrot!" He also barks every time we put him outside because he is territorial. He takes this role very seriously even when the mail person that comes at the same time every day shows up to deliver the mail! He has very little discernment and I try to talk to him about it, but he just looks at me and then eventually lays back down.

Often, we think he is going crazy or declining. Other times, we think he is intentionally not learning anything from us. The only trick we have taught him is the go around the tree maneuver to untangle his chain when he goes out to pee. He learned lots of tricks from someone else, but he refuses to learn anything new from me. It just makes us both anxious to try to learn new tricks, so we eventually just go back to our recliners. That's right, he has his own recliner! He's very sensitive to some foods and especially frightened of storms. He even seems to be able to anticipate that a storm is coming. But the thing Winston the Wonder Dog does best is just being who he is.

Maybe a lot of our stress is that we don't know who we are. How much of our waking hours is devoted to trying to reinvent ourselves or build our logo or brand instead of just being who we are? What if we knew, from deep inside us, who we are, and we just lived authentically from that place?

There are some things about Winston that are common to most dogs. The characteristic people use to describe most dogs are loyalty and unconditional love. People use other words like faithful to describe them, but most of the descriptions mean about the same thing. Winston is happy greeting us, being with us and anticipating our return. As far as I know, he is relatively happy just being around us. When extended family or friends come over, he receives their affection, but he doesn't miss them like he misses us. This loyalty is probably one of the main reasons we like dogs.

I was thinking yesterday about this premise. I have always been somewhat of an introvert and I have never had a lot of close friends. Also, Laura reminds me that when I complete a task, I am usually quickly on to the next task. I think I am also like this with people. Once I make a friend online, I am quickly on to finding another friend. If one friend is good, two is probably better. Some people are like this with pets and they accumulate more than they can handle. But dogs seem content to just have about one or two friends in life because they are loyal. What if I were more like Winston and just devoted more attention to people that are already in my life? It's okay to have a broader influence, but better to be faithful with what I have now.

I don't know if dogs mentally think about forgiveness, but they seem to be good at it. Maybe their memory is less advanced than ours or maybe their love for us is more important than keeping score. Sometimes I yell at Winston when he doesn't do things like I expect. He will cower a little or just go sit in his chair. Unfortunately, I feel like I'm doing my duty to mold him, but if I am honest, it's just my pride or my ego that needs to have control. Sometimes, it seems like he is pouting about it, but really, I think he is just waiting for me to get over it. If I throw him the ball or pat him on the head, he is just as happy as if it never happened.

Currently, we are going through a crisis with the COVID-19 virus. We have simplified our meal plans because we can't go out much and we can't run to the store to get special items every day. We usually go to the store about once a week. Even with this restriction, we still eat a wide variety of things because I get bored eating the same thing every day. But Winston does not seem to be bothered by this. We give him a carrot and an ice cube once a day as a treat. We feed him the same dog food every day and his tale starts to wag every time we put it in the bowl. He seems to be grateful. Maybe, he doesn't have any choice, but that's probably part of the point.

I don't know what dogs think about. Sometimes I hear Winston have a dream. He seems to be wrestling with something in his sleep. Maybe that's true of all sentient beings—if there is memory and brain function, it must reset and process through what needs to be retained—or something like that. He seems to be thinking about things, especially when I say a word that he has never heard before. But there is one thing I have never observed him doing—he never is mentally somewhere else when I speak to him—he is always present! Maybe it is because he doesn't have a smartphone, but I don't think so. He is always here even when there is nothing to do. He realizes doing nothing together is still doing something. I seriously long to be more present like my dog.

At the end of the day, Winston seems very content to know that he lived authentically. He ate the food that he had and asked for a couple of carrots and ice cubes. When I give him too many carrots, he just leaves the other one on the floor. He barked at the mail person because that is what dogs do. His warning call is alarming, and Laura is happy that he sounds fierce when I'm not home. He rolled around on the floor and exercised a little (played with the ball), chewed on his bone a little, stretched out a couple of times, and drank water out of the toilet. But he didn't get obsessive or excessive about any of it and He didn't regret that he did almost the exact same things the next day. At the end of day, he follows us to bed knowing that he did what was normal for a dog of his breed.

As humans, we often honor and long for the exceptional. We want to stand out from the crowd—to be recognized by our peers—to excel. But being who we are is exceptional in and of itself. Maybe this is called contentment—maybe it's authenticity—but it's certainly not a compromise. Being who we are may be our single greatest accomplishment in life. I hope to be more like Winston, but only to the extent that I act more like me.

What I Learned from Winston

by Karl Forehand

I often think my dog is crazy,
    cause' he does the same things each day.
But then I think about it closely,
    And I see faithfulness in his way

I often think my dog is lazy,
    cause' he doesn't learn any new skills.
But then I think about it closely,
    and I see contentment in his will.

I often think my dog is simple,
    cause' he doesn't long for what he's not.
But then I think about it closely,
    And I see the beauty of his plot.

I often think my dog is pesky,
    cause' he rushes at me from the floor.
But then I think about it closely,
    and I see love for those he adores.

I often think my dog is too gruff,
    cause' he barks at the same ones each day.
But then I think about it closely,
    and I understand his protective ways.

I often think my dog is distant,
    cause' he is just not at all verbose.
But then I think about it closely,
    and I feel love as he snuggles up close.

BEING WITH MY BODY

We get all kinds of mixed messages from society and religion. My tradition taught that my body was a temple, but it also stressed that it was some sort of evil machine that just thought about sex all the time and could not really control itself. Sometimes they stressed it was like a tent to carry around the more spiritual or soulful part of me, but it was also the "flesh" that was the source of all my sin. The body was considered something that was dying and would not last into eternity—and eternity was what mattered.

In junior high, when I would have had sex education, we attended a Christian school that was of the mindset that we did not talk about things like that. This sexual nature of my body I discovered soon enough on my own. I did not have any reference points for good information, and we did not have google at that time, so I mostly got bad information. But what I was discovering did not seem bad. It was good—it was incredibly good. Occasionally, I would ponder the complexity of the body's systems when I would learn about them in a science class or in a documentary on television. Even a simple erection, points to a complex system of nerves and blood flow that boggles the mind to consider. But I was not really thinking about that at the time, if you know what I mean. Eventually, I just stopped thinking about how the body is designed because it did not seem relevant or useful at the time.

But, later as I was participating in a spiritual formation experience with a group of Sisters in Atchison, Kansas, I came across something unusual. As we would sit in groups, we would take turns listening to each other. Sometimes it is called group spiritual direction. They taught us to listen deeply and try to experience how the Divine was interacting with all of us. This was like when I took Spiritual Leadership Coaching classes and they taught us to listen for the Spirit. This made sense to me and was a part of my basic beliefs. But then the Sisters and group leaders began to teach us something else that I later learned was discovered in the 70's.

When someone would tell a story about how they were feeling or what they wanted to examine, the director (or companion) would ask them to describe the emotion they were feeling. Recently, I have learned to help people express this examination of emotion as "a part of me feels … "[15] But, then they did something I did not understand. They would say, "where in your body do you feel that?" It would be much later that I would learn the significance of that simple statement. Without writing another book to explain this, please allow me to simply state that our bodies store much of our trauma. We like to think of it as a mind thing, but to me it seems like a much more organic thing. When we can be with that part of us that holds the trauma, we can begin to heal and remove the stuck places in our experience.

This is what happened in the recliner at the hermitage. I did not really understand what I was doing (and I still do not totally). But, when I "focused" on the feeling that was stored there, it took me back to a current sense of what I experienced in the past. My friend, Dr. Paul, is teaching me to be with that part of me that was once wounded and have compassion for my inner child and my inner critic as well.[16] I

---

15 Dr. Paul Fitzgerald, HCS Focusing, https://heartconnexion.thinkific.com/
16 Ibid.

have had multiple experience of being with those parts of me and even helped some others to focus and learn from their bodies.

I wish I would have paid more attention in science class because now I am learning that body awareness can vastly improve our experience as humans. Eugene Gendlin talks about a physical experience we can have of bodily awareness that not only informs us but can change our lives. When this "felt sense" of a situation changes, then our lives can change for the better.[17] I would encourage people to consult a spiritual director or counselor that has experience with this type of therapy. It is one of the most exciting trends I see on the horizon.

I have learned to care for my body and to listen to it. Ignoring anything hardly never makes it better. Our bodies have messages for us. When we feel anxiety in our gut, it is not always the pizza we had the night before. Often, it is past experiences and trauma that need our attention. We do not have to exorcise or remove the things that trouble us necessarily. Most often we probably just need to take the role of the observer and be compassionate. We do not need to belittle or bypass the issue, but we also do not need to beat it into submission. We need to be with it and understand it; and then, most often, when we can be sympathetic to it, the felt sense of it shifts and our lives improve.

Right now, we are caring for Winston, our dog. He has a hotspot on his torso that could be from skin irritation or maybe even anxiety. He constantly licks the inflamed area and it just continues to get worse and worse. We had to put a neck pillow on him so he would not mess with it and we spray it with something we got from the vet. This is

---

17   Gendlin, E.T., (2007). *Focussing*, New York: Bantam Dell, 27

obvious because we can see it, but much our trauma lies stored in our bodies. Occasionally, it itches, and we scratch it too hard or we just try to ignore it, but maybe what it needs is some fresh air. The analogy breaks down and it does not always make sense. But we certainly cannot ignore it. The things we stored inside do not go away, and often they come back with a vengeance and behave in unpredictable ways. Just like heart disease can be a silent killer, emotional trauma that is unaddressed can ruin us if we do not address it.

I hope modern advances in science will help me even better understand body awareness like I understand other ailments. I hope I can learn to be with myself and learn to observe with compassion what I see there. I want to practice self-care and not feel selfish. I want to appreciate and honor the complex, wonderful and amazing body that I have as I also nurture and care for it. Just like I eat a plant-based diet and exercise for my health, I hope to engage in practices that help me be present and observe disruption in my body's emotions.

With that, I wish to issue you a final challenge!

EPILOGUE—BRAVERY AND VULNERABILITY

"Vulnerability sounds like truth and feels like courage. Truth and courage aren't always comfortable, but they are never weakness."

BRENÉ BROWN [18]

I would have loved to write this book just about being. I would have loved to give you a simple little mantra or a practice that would revolutionize your life. But life does not work that way! The things that happen to us and the things that happen around us affect us greatly and we are often left with unfinished business. That work that must be done is sort of like the small trees growing in my gutters. I caught a glimpse of them the other day and I quickly looked away. But they are still there, and my gutters do not work properly. They will not work right until I borrow a ladder and do the uncomfortable, dirty work of cleaning out years of accumulated debris.

What keeps me from simply being is probably like things that hinder you. Well-meaning people cause trauma for us that leave wounds and stoppages in us. The longer we ignore these things, the worse they seem to misbehave when they break out. We have a life of experience with doing some things the wrong way. We were once convinced that our confidence and energy would get us through, but we have grown weary and lost hope that thing will change. We often feel things like despair and depression and then we bypass or minimize what our bodies are trying to tell us.

---

18 https://bookriot.com/2018/04/16/brene-brown-quotes/

But then we summon up the courage to be brave. We hear a new technique to overcome our weaknesses. We learn about a device or a pill or a process that is guaranteed to provide results. We muster up our confidence and we give it one last try. But, at the end of the day or week or month, we are more discouraged than when we begin. Why? Because, the sister of courage and bravery is to be vulnerable. And vulnerability is not comfortable to anyone. It is like walking outdoors naked for most of us. It is like when the first punch lands in a boxing match and of the contestants feels that feeling in the pit of their stomach. It is telling them; you are in danger—this might go bad—this is going to hurt!

I felt it when I tried to overcome my fear of public speaking. I was trying to give an extemporaneous speech in front of a few colleagues. Just a minute, not a big deal! After 10-15 seconds, my mind was swimming, my face was flushed, and I felt like I was going to pass out. Bravery made me vulnerable. Courage meant the most likely next thing I was going to feel is like I am exposed—and I was! Most of the stories I told myself were untrue—I was not going to die, they were not laughing at me, I did not sound stupid. My brain was just off on a rampage, somehow trying to protect me from a danger that was not there.

We cannot get around vulnerability. The focusing sessions I do or participate in seem like the easiest thing to avoid, because I'm going to be physically exhausted afterwards, I'm probably going to cry and it is literally going to be painful to examine trauma and dysfunction in my life. I hate to say it, but it is hard work! I often say the most important thing about a job or business is to show up for work. It is true! Most problems and performance issues can be worked through if the person will be there on the appointed days. So, that is what I tell myself these days about the self-care I need to do, just go to work—I know it is not easy, but it is always worth it!

I encourage you to take the next courageous step. The journey that surrounds this book is approximately a 3-year journey. Beneath that, are almost 20 years of trying to understand how humans work and what God is like and how all that matters. There are very few things about my deconstruction or shadow work that were easy, but it has all been worth it. Being where I am and being who I am did not happen overnight and I still have work to do, but I look forward to the next chapters that will be written!

Peace be with you!

– Karl

Connect with Karl Forehand

- ✉ karl@karlforehand.com
- f @KarlForehandAuthor
- 🐦 @karl4hand

Shaia-Sophia House is a collaborative effort of Alexander John Shaia and Nora Sophia's passion to provide a creative home for fresh works from the great traditions. We begin as a publishing house with plans to expand soon into various mediums.

www.ShaiaSophiaHouse.com

www.ingramcontent.com/pod-product-compliance
Lightning Source LLC
Chambersburg PA
CBHW031115080526
44587CB00011B/981